# *Mike Storms' Parenting 101*

## A PRACTICAL HANDS-ON GUIDE TO RAISING REMARKABLE KIDS

PRESS LLC

SANFORD • FLORIDA

Published by: DC Press, LLC, 2445 River Tree Circle, Sanford, FL32271, www.focusonethics.com or www.dcpressbooks.com



Unless otherwise noted, italics and bold treatment used in Scriptures and quotes indicate the author's added emphasis.

EDITOR AND CONCEPT DEVELOPMENT:

Vincent M. Newfield v New Fields & Company v P.O. Box 622 v Hillsboro, Missouri 63050 v www.preparethewaytoday.org

TEXT DESIGN: Debra Deysher
COVER DESIGN: Stephanie Katz

ISBN: 978-1-932021-67-7
Printed in USA
10 9 8 7 6 5 4 3 2 1

# Dedication

*This book is dedicated*
*to the*
*Audience of One,*
*that turned*
*a lost and broken man*
*into a son.*

## *Appreciation for...*

My wife, Glori, I will be forever grateful to God for allowing me the privilege of being your husband, protector, provider and best friend. You are my greatest earthly blessing. There would be no Mike Storms' ***Parenting 101*** without your belief in this project, encouragement, and hard work proofing and editing. You are a faithful, loyal, kind, godly woman. I am amazed by you.

My children: Austin, Jake, Jessica, and Shea. You all bring a song to my heart. Thanks for helping with this project over your entire lifetimes!

A special thanks to my parents, mentors, friends, coaches and students that have taught me so much. You are in all of the pages of this book. It would of been impossible to write without your input and guidance over my lifetime. A special thank you to my spiritual father, and dear friend, Keith Hafner for always having the time for me and being available, and for your unwavering support and confidence in me. Also , thank you to those who gave feedback along the way. Bill Magee and Elizabeth Storms for your proofing help.

To Vincent Newfield for his talents, who believed in this message and worked tirelessly to organize and help in writing of this project. Thank you for your powerful prayers, guidance and encouragement. Thanks to Dennis McClellan for his professionalism and guidance on this project.

Most importantly , my deepest gratitude and love to our Father in Heaven, for His son Jesus Christ, and for His forgiveness, grace, and love, and to the Holy Spirit for His guidance and comfort and peace during this entire project.

Michael B. Storms
Mandeville, LA

# Table of Contents

# Chapter 1

# *Understanding How Your Kids Are Shaped*

"Direct your children onto the right path, and when they are older, they will not leave it."

—Proverbs 22:6 NLT

Excellent, happy, healthy children — that's the dream of every parent. Unleashing our children's full potential and motivating them to choose the right path is our deepest desire. We want to see them grow into confident, kind, and loving people —people who serve God and change the world for good. The question is, "How do we do it?" How do we raise our children to be happy, successful, and responsible? What must we do to ensure that they don't grow up weak-willed, whiny, and self-centered?

Thankfully, there is an answer. There are specific things we can do to train our children to be a blessing to us and to others.

As a martial arts instructor for 27 years, I have had the privilege of working with over 6,000 kids and their parents. I am also raising four children of my own, and I don't hesitate to admit that I am not a perfect parent or teacher. Like you, I've made my share of mistakes. But through my experience and the study of great parenting wisdom, I have discovered three major influencers that shape the lives of all children—things that mold them in either a positive or a negative way. These influencers are the *media*, their *friends*, and *parental example.*

By understanding how these influencers work and harnessing their power for good, we can raise our kids to become champions of truth that are actively engaged in shaping society.

There are three main influencers that shape the lives of all children. They are the *media* they consume, the *friends* they hang out with, and the *parental example* lived before them.

## Manage Their Media Menu

The first major influence we must recognize is the media. Without question, today's entertainment has taken center stage in the lives of many people. The number one thing to remember about the media is: ***input equals output***. What enters your children's eyes and ears comes out in their behavior, character and attitudes. The Bible says in Proverbs 4:23 (NIV), "Above all else, guard your heart, for it is the wellspring of life". Your eyes and ears are the doors to your heart. So every movie and TV show your children watch, every video game they play, every Internet site they surf, every song they hear, and every magazine and book they read is going to affect them in either a positive or negative way. There is no neutral.

When I was a kid growing up, the TV set was often called the "idiot box" because, as the story goes, when a person watched too much TV, they turned into an idiot. It's estimated that children today watch an average of twenty-eight to thirty-two hours of television a week.[1] Add in surfing the Internet and playing video games, and the hours children spend engaged in electronic media climbs to nearly fifty-five hours a week.[2] This is more time than they spend in school, in extracurricular activities, in church and in some cases, it is even more hours than they sleep in a week! Media will be the biggest influence on your children, simply because it gets the most attention from your children.

> Every movie and TV show your kids watch, every video game they play, every Internet site they surf, and every magazine and book they read is going to affect them in either a positive or negative way. There is no neutral.

So, what values are your children learning through the media? By showcasing beautiful people in beautiful surroundings, living exciting, dramatic lives the media can create a discontent with our looks, our clothes, our car, our house, and even our spouse. Children learn from the media, that if you want to be happy and important, you must be good-looking, rich and popular. If you want to know why your kids want new toys, new clothes, and a new hair style, or why they think that they are too fat or too skinny, or not good-looking enough, take a look at what they are watching and listening to. You can be sure that the messages being presented by the mainstream media almost always contradict the message of Jesus' Sermon on the Mount[3] and the apostle Paul's statement to the church at Philippi about being content in all circumstances.[4]

The media also affects our children's behavior. While counseling concerned parents whose children were exhibiting poor behavior, I have often been able to trace back the child's inappropriate actions to the antics of a character on a TV show the child was watching regularly, or to a video game they were playing. Even many of the characters on so-called "family friendly" programs leave a lot to be desired. In most of the sitcoms, the father is portrayed as a moron and the mom is in charge of everything. The scripts are written in such a way that the children seem to know it all, have little or no respect for their parents, and the plot often revolves around the children deceiving their parents to try to stay out of trouble. We can't expect our kids to act appropriately and respectfully if they are watching "cool" kids on TV and in movies act inappropriately and disrespectfully. Like a mirror, they will reflect the images they see modeled before them.

We can't expect our kids to act appropriately and respectfully if they are watching "cool" kids on TV and in movies act inappropriately and disrespectfully. Like a mirror, they will reflect the images they see modeled before them.

What can make matters worse is the content of television commercials. I have been astonished to see racy lingerie commercials aired during shows that are geared toward families. Also, R rated movies and lewd TV shows are promoted during primetime hours when children are most likely to be watching. In our home, we initially trained our kids to turn their heads or cover their faces when something inappropriate came on. We even taught them to start singing loudly with their hands over their ears until we could change the channel. Eventually, we came to the point where we chose to stop watching some channels altogether, whose shows and commercials had become outrageously out of line.

As standards of decency have worsened, we've made a decision to nix broadcast TV completely and just buy or rent our own DVDs. By creating a library of wholesome entertainment, you can eliminate the influence of crazy commercials and take control regarding what your kids are watching.

## So How Much Media Are Your Kids Consuming?

The most important thing you can do is to control the quality and quantity of media your children consume. You are the policeman -- you are the one with the authority over what comes into your house. You are responsible for what your children watch and hear.

This is important: Don't let them watch television or movies unless you are watching with them to monitor the content. Listen to their music with them and preview their video games. Read their books before they do. If the images they are seeing and the words they are hearing and reading are not the kind you want to see reproduced in their behavior, change the input. Cut out the negative and replace it with positive alternatives. You can check out some healthy media menu options in the back of my - *Parenting 101 Workbook.*

As for *quantity*, begin to limit your children's TV intake to a handful of hours a week. This rule can also be applied to playing video games, spending time on the Internet, and listening to music. For my family, I set a boundary early on, not allowing the children to play video games until they were in second or third grade. When they did play, they were given only an hour per person on Saturdays. No video games or TV were allowed during the school week. As the children got older, I increased the time for playing video games up to two hours, but they still could not play during the school week. When they became upperclassmen in high school, they were allowed to watch television for about an hour a day as long as their grades were excellent. Create a media schedule that works for your family based on the age, maturity and responsibility level of each of your children.

Another thing I highly recommend is having only *one* TV and computer and placing them in the living room or family room—not in your children's bedroom. This helps eliminate distractions in the children's studying and sleeping areas, decreases their risk of seeing inappropriate images without you knowing about it, and creates opportunities for everyone to come together and watch a good, family-friendly movie. It also prevents electronic entertainment from becoming the main focus of your family's time. I also strongly suggest having Internet and TV filters to protect your children from accidental exposure to inappropriate material.

> Begin monitoring the *quality* and *quantity* of media that is coming into your home. If the images your children are seeing and the words they are hearing and reading are not the kind you want to see reproduced in their behavior, change the input.

## Filter the Friends Your Kids Hang Out With

Another major influence that shapes the lives of your children is their *friends*. I always tell my students, "Show me your friends and I'll show you your future." Your kids will rise or fall to the expectations of their peers. If they hang out with poorly behaved children, who often get into trouble and have no real direction in life, they will begin to exhibit the same behavior. On the other hand, if they hang out with peers who are walking on the right road, they will be motivated to live the right way.

The Bible has a number of things to say about the company we keep. First Corinthians 15:33 (NIV) says, "Do not be misled: 'Bad company corrupts good character'," and how true it is. Think about it - if you spend a lot of time around people who are sick, you are going to catch what they have. This is why God says, "Don't become partners with those who reject God. How can you make a partnership out of right and wrong? That's not partnership; that's war. Is light best friends with dark? Does Christ go strolling with the Devil? Do trust and mistrust hold hands?"[5] You probably already know that the answer is "Absolutely not!"

> Show me your friends and I'll show you your future. If your kids hang out with ungodly children, they will begin to exhibit the same behavior. On the other hand, if they hang out with positive peers, they will be motivated to live the right way.

I have four children; three of them are young adults and one is in elementary school. My concern about who they become friends with has remained strong throughout their lives. For years I have had certain standards that my children's friends must meet. Some of the questions I ask my kids about a potential friend are, "What kind of grades do they make? Do they play sports or have an activity they are passionate about? What kind of movies and music do they watch and listen to? What kind of books and magazines do they read? Where do they go to church?" As my kids got older, I included some other questions like, "Do they have a job? What do they want to do with their life? Do they drink or smoke or do drugs? How is their relationship with God?" If they weren't the kind of kids that I wanted my kids to be like, I would not let them associate with them. Period.

Now, if you are thinking, *Mike, you're too controlling...you're too particular. I can't do that with my kids.* I would urge you to rethink your position. Just as you need to screen the media your kids consume, you must also filter the friends they spend time with.

Prolonged exposure to unruly, rebellious kids leads to contamination. You've probably heard your grandmother say "Lie down with dogs and you're going to get fleas." It is just as true today as it was in grandma's time. If your children hang around kids who lie, cheat, and steal, guess what they are going to eventually do? If they associate with kids who are self-centered, disrespectful to their parents, and rebel against authority, guess how they are going to start acting? The Bible confirms this, saying, "Make no friendship with an angry man, and with a furious man do not go, *lest you learn his ways* and set a snare for your soul" (Proverbs 22:24,25 NKJV).

Just as you need to screen the media your kids consume, you must also filter the friends they spend their time with. Prolonged exposure to unruly, rebellious kids leads to contamination. If you lie down with dogs, you're going to get fleas.

The *ways* you want your children to learn are *godly* ways. Consequently, they need to be spending time with godly kids who are developing godly character. The Bible says, "As iron sharpens iron, so a friend sharpens a friend" (Proverbs 27:17 NLT). Look for kids whose parents are actively involved in their lives, helping them grow and mature in a healthy way. Now, I want to make it clear that not all church-going children are raised equally. That is, there are a number of kids who go to church with their parents, but their lives are really no different than the non-church-going children. The statistics on divorce and premarital sex among Christians proves this. Therefore, do some background checks on your children's choice of friends. Invite them and their parents over for a meal and watch how they interact with each other. It won't take long to see the true measure of their character. All you need to do is monitor the words of their mouth. In due time, they will speak out of the abundance of what is in their heart.[6]

I realize you may be thinking, Mike, are you saying my kids can never hang out with kids who need help? No, that is not what I am saying. I believe that we should reach out to kids who are in trouble and try to give them a hand up. We should offer them the truth through mentoring and counseling. However, we need to limit our kids' exposure to them, and our children must understand why we are involved. One benefit this type of relationship provides for your children is an example of what wrong choices will produce. It can be a warning to your children to avoid making the same mistakes. And at the same time, it is also a bridge of hope to the troubled child—a lifeline of God's love that may one day connect them in relationship with the Creator of the universe who can truly transform their life into something awesome. But you must constantly monitor the relationship to ensure that your kids are the influencers and not the influenced.

God has placed you in your children's lives for a brief amount of time. He has commissioned you to train them up in the way they should go, and that training includes teaching them how to choose good friends—friends who will motivate them to do right and fulfill their God-given destiny. Proverbs 13:20 in The Message says, "Become wise by walking with the wise; hang out with fools and watch your life fall to pieces." It all comes down to helping our children make right choices so that when they are adults they will have the wisdom and skills to choose wisely for themselves.

> God has placed you in your children's lives for a brief amount of time. He has commissioned you to train them up in the way they should go, and that training includes teaching them how to choose good friends—friends who will motivate them to do right and fulfill their God-given destiny.

## Live the Life You Want Them to Live

The third and most important influence in your children's lives is *you.* The example you live before your children each day impresses a blueprint for living onto their hearts and minds that is not easily altered. The things you say, how you respond to adversity, the way you love and serve the Lord—you are constantly teaching and your children are always learning. As a parent, your actions speak louder than your instruction. So how are you living? God's Word says, "He who heeds instruction and correction is [not only himself] in the way of life [but also] **is a way of life** for others. And he who neglects or refuses reproof [not only himself] goes astray [but also] causes to err and *is a path toward ruin* for others" (Proverbs 10:17

AMP). Wow! Our actions are either *a way of life* for our children or *a path toward ruin.* The choices you make and the actions you take pave a path for your kids to walk on.

> As a parent, your actions speak louder than words. The example you live before your children each day impresses a blueprint for living onto their hearts and minds that is not easily altered.

## What Kind of Example Are You *Seeding*?

Basically, all of our attitudes and actions are *seeds* we plant in the lives of others, and our children are the greatest recipients of these seeds. The Bible gives us a sobering principle in Galatians 6:7,8. It says, "...What a person plants, he will harvest. The person who plants selfishness, ignoring the needs of others—ignoring God!—harvests a crop of weeds. All he'll have to show for his life is weeds! But the one who plants in response to God, letting God's Spirit do the growth work in him, harvests a crop of real life, eternal life" (The Message). The behavior we see in our children is, to a great degree, the harvest from the seeds we have been planting in their lives for weeks, months, and years. When counseling families, I am no longer surprised to find that the behavior the parents are most concerned about in their children is behavior that the parents themselves exhibit.

For example, take your attitude toward those in authority over you. When you have had a rough day at work, do you come home and bad-mouth your boss? When you see government leaders make wrong decisions, do you criticize and cut them down in the presence of your family? If a police officer pulls you over for not coming to a full stop at a stop sign, what kind of things do your kids hear you say about him after you get back on the road? If you judge, criticize, and disrespect people in authority in front of your kids, they will do the same thing to the people in authority over them. When their teacher, coach, or even you do something they don't like, they will respond in the same way that was modeled before them. As in every area of your life, your example of rebellion and disrespect **or** submission and honor are seeds being planted in their lives. In time, a harvest will come.

Basically, our attitudes and actions are *seeds* we plant in the lives of others, and our children are the greatest recipients of these seeds. The behavior we see in them is, to a great degree, the harvest from the seeds we have been planting in their lives for weeks, months, and years.

One of my dear friends and his wife recently had their first child – a beautiful baby boy. Upon receiving the birth announcement, I responded to him with this message: "Now you will be even further transformed by the influence of your son's expectations of you." Our kids have an amazing way of humbling us and challenging us to become better people—if we let them. Each of my children has motivated me to become a better man. Their complete trust in and reliance on me, as well as their belief in me as Super Dad inspires me to continuously develop my character. I want to be the wise, loving father that they need. But before I could be an example of excellence, I needed to put first things first and get my life right with God.

## The Most Important Example You Can Give

The most important thing we can model for our children is an always deepening, personal relationship with God. By attending and serving in church, having daily private devotions with God, trusting in His Word, and putting Him first in all that we do, God enables us not only to be all that He created us to be, but also to give our children a close-up, living example of the Christian faith. We should make seeking God's help to walk closer with Him our top priority. The apostle Paul said it well when he stated, "Everything else is worthless when compared with the priceless gain of knowing Christ Jesus my Lord. I have put aside all else, counting it worth less than nothing, in order that I can have Christ, and become one with him..." (Philippians 3:8,9 TLB).

Without complete and total surrender to Christ, we are powerless to live the example before our kids that they need.[7] As we give ourselves over to Him daily, He will begin to change the way we talk, the way we think, and the way we act. Bad habits and ungodly desires will begin to melt away and be replaced with godly ones. It is God who will "strengthen (complete, perfect) and make you what you ought to be and equip you with everything good that you may carry out His will..." (Hebrews 13:21 AMP). Instead of our behavior being a path toward ruin for our kids, it will be a pathway of life!

The example of our own faith can lead our children to the most important decision they can make – to accept Jesus Christ as their Lord and Savior and to live for Him. When we are obedient to God's command to impress upon our children the commandments He has given us[8] and they see us grow in our relationship with Him and experience the blessing of His promises, they will be drawn by His loving kindness to the throne of grace. We must provide the antidote for the worldly beliefs that are being pushed onto our kids all the time.

Think about it. Many kids spend seven to eight hours a day at public school being influenced by their peers and the warped philosophies of man. Then they come home and feed on a few hours of wordly media. At best, some of these kids go to church once on Sunday and maybe once during the week. Is it any wonder they are struggling with purity and rebellion when we're only inoculating them with an hour or two of truth each week while they're getting over one hundred hours of everything else shoved down their throats? Clearly, what our kids need is a firsthand, personal relationship with God, and this starts with your example.

> The greatest thing you and I can do as parents is to surrender our lives to God and serve Him with all our heart. Without Him, we are powerless to live the godly example before our kids that they need.

## With God, You've Got What It Takes!

If you want your kids to get better, *you've* got to get better, and the only way to truly get better is by completely surrendering your life Jesus Christ. Not only will He make you a new creation[9] , but He will also enable you to carry out His parenting principles. Being a parent is the toughest job there is and at times it can seem overwhelming, but with the Creator of the Universe on your side, you've got what it takes! Find rest in 2 Corinthians 12:9 which says, "My grace is sufficient for you, for my power is made perfect in weakness." He will enable you to stand tall and make the tough and unpopular choices for your children's sake. I encourage you to make a commitment before God to deepen your relationship with Him. He has promised in James 4:8 (NKJV) that He will meet us as we seek more of Him; "Draw near to God, and He will draw near to you".

If you have never invited Jesus Christ into your heart and are not sure where you stand with God, turn to page 247 for some good news!

**TAKE AWAY**

- WHAT ARE THE TOP 3 NUGGETS OF WISDOM YOU CAN TAKE AWAY FROM THIS CHAPTER?
- WHAT PRINCIPLES ARE YOU ALREADY DOING?
- WHICH ONES DO YOU NEED TO PRAY AND ASK GOD TO HELP YOU PUT INTO PRACTICE?

---

**PARENTING 101 RECAP**: To understand how your kids are shaped, you must understand the three major influences in their lives: the *media* they consume, the *friends* they hang out with, and the *example* you live before them. By controlling the quality and quantity of media they receive, helping them pick and partner with virtuous peers, and living the kind of life before them that you know is best, you can begin to positively impact the lives of your children. This is the foundation for raising happy, healthy, godly kids that are world changers.

# Chapter 2

## *Harnessing the Power Of Your Words*

"Death and life are in the power of the tongue, and those who love it will eat its fruit."

—Proverbs 18:21 NKJV

Genesis 1 gives us a detailed account of how God created the heavens and the earth. At least eight times the words "and God *said*" appear in the chapter, linking His creative power to His words. He didn't just *think* the universe into existence—He *spoke* it into existence. Romans 4:17 (NASB) confirms this, saying that God "...gives life to the dead and *calls into being* that which does not exist." In a similar way, our words have creative power. Since *you* are the most powerful influence in your children's lives, the words you speak to them carry great weight and define who they become. Like the hands of a master potter, your words mold and shape them into a person of worth and honor or a person of dishonor with little or no value. The Scripture says that we are created in the image of God, and that we are to imitate Him like a child imitates his father.[1] Just as God spoke and brought forth life and order to the universe, we are to speak and bring forth life and order to our children.

## Choose Your Words Wisely

We live in a culture of criticism full of grumbling, fault-finding and complaining. People seem to effortlessly gravitate toward the negative. For instance, if we went to a restaurant and had a bad experience, we would probably go on-and-on about it to everyone we know, but if we had a great experience, we might forget to mention it at all. This focus on the negative spills over into our parenting. We point out every character flaw our children have and neglect to tell them about their wonderful qualities. Our lectures about their bad behavior go on for ten minutes, but often when they do something good, we say nothing or simply "good job." As Dale Carnegie says, "We must be lavish with our praise."

One of the most wonderful and scary things about our kids is that they believe what we say to them and about them—especially when they are young. They do not have a filter to sort out that which is untrue or destructive to their self esteem and character. *We* paint our children's self-portrait on the canvas of their mind and they become what we repeatedly tell them they are. This means that the behavior you are getting from your kids is in part the harvest of what you have seeded over and over again with your words.

If your child is struggling in school and you say, "I don't know if you'll ever get this, you never listen," you'll get a kid that doubts their intelligence and believes that they are not a good listener. Angry, critical words destroy self-esteem and create doubts about their abilities and value well into adulthood. There is no clearer verse in the Bible that confirms this than Proverbs 18:21. In The Message Bible you'll find, "Words kill, words give life; they're either poison or fruit – you choose." Every day as you open your mouth and speak to your children, you are choosing to be either in the demolition or construction business.

You must choose your words wisely.

> Since *you* are the most powerful influence in your children's lives, the words you speak to them carry great weight and *define* who they become. The behavior you are getting from them is the harvest of what you have seeded over and over again with your words. You must choose your words wisely.

The Bible says, "Whoever of you loves life and desires to see many good days, keep your tongue from evil and your lips from telling lies. Turn from evil and do good; seek peace and pursue it" (Psalm 34:12-14 NIV). If we love our lives and want to see many good days, we need to get control of our tongue. Learning to control what we say is a process. Like any other muscle of the body, our tongue must be brought under control through exercise, which, in this case, is developing the habit of saying the right thing and not saying the wrong thing.

If you realize your words have been harsh and hurtful toward your children, don't feel condemned. God will help you change if you let Him. Instead of just griping and complaining about the wrong behavior you see, He will prompt you to begin "calling into being those things which do not exist" as though they did. He will empower you to begin painting a new self-portrait on the canvas of their hearts and minds.

## Break the Pattern of Poor Parenting

So, if your words pack the most punch in your kids' lives, the words of your parents or the people who raised you have greatly defined the person and parent you have become. When I was growing up, the words I heard from my father were very negative. Phrases like, "You're too small," "You can't do it," and "You're such an idiot," were often hurled at my head in anger and disappointment. Words like these greatly affected what I thought of myself and what I felt I was capable of accomplishing. Amazingly, even many years later, I can still sometimes hear phrases like this echo in my mind.

My father grew up in New York during the Great Depression, and he had a father who was very hard on him. So, my father hurt me because his father had hurt him. That is what often happens in families. The pattern of pain is perpetuated from one generation to the next. I believe this is what God meant when He said, "...I lay the sins of the parents upon their children; *the entire family is affected*—even children in the third and fourth generations of those who reject me" (Exodus 20:5 NLT). Thankfully, He doesn't leave us there in despair but goes on to say in the very next verse, "But I lavish unfailing love for a thousand generations on those who love me and obey my commands."

Once someone *hears* and *believes* the life-changing message of truth—that through Jesus Christ we are free to live a new and improved life—the pattern of poor parenting can be broken. This was the case with me. I knew I didn't want to repeat many of the things I had experienced as a kid. I resolved to go in the opposite direction of my father and use my words to build a bright future for my children. But without God, my progress was slow and no matter how hard I tried, I still often exploded in anger. When I accepted Jesus Christ as my Savior, he began to heal the wounds of my childhood and enable me to overcome my temper. By the power of God and the help of some great mentors (and a lot of prayer), I have been able to shake off most of the negativity that was deposited in my life and not repeat the parenting patterns of my family.

> Once someone *hears* and *believes* the life-changing message of truth—that through Jesus Christ we are free to live a new and improved life—the pattern of poor parenting can be broken.

If your parents' words toward you were not positive, you too can choose to go in the opposite direction. By the power of God, you can break the pattern of poor parenting. Realize that this is a process that may take some time.

As you seek the Lord, He will remove the sting of the wounding words that ring in your ears. Instead of speaking the same kind of cutting comments you heard, He will help you change your vocabulary with wonderful words of life so that your conversation will "...be always full of grace, seasoned with salt, so that you may know how to answer everyone,"[2] including your kids!

## Seven Things You can do to Harness the Power of Your Words

Now that we have firmly established the effects of negative, hurtful words, let's take a look at seven specific things you can begin doing to harness the power of your words. These include replacing the negative with positive, becoming a good listener, keeping the lines of communication open, learning to speak your kids' love language, watching your nonverbal expressions, starting and ending the day on a good note, and being willing to say "I'm sorry," when you mess up.

## Replace the Negative with Positive

Once you begin to recognize and eliminate the negative words you have been speaking to your kids, you need to *replace* them with positive ones. When parents tell me they are going to stop saying negative things, I remind them that they must also start saying positive things or the negative will come back in full force. Nature hates a vacuum—the void must be filled. Therefore, you must find ways to praise your kids and be a source of strength that nurtures their positive development. The Bible says, "The right word at the right time is like a custom-made piece of jewelry" (Proverbs 25:11 The Message). Positive words of encouragement help to make your children shine brightly, building their confidence and security. It's really quite simple, "If mommy and daddy think I have what it takes, I must!"

Many parents have a hard time saying positive, encouraging things to their children. For some it feels unnatural and uncomfortable. This is especially true if it is not something they heard while growing up. For others, they think giving their kids praise will cause them to become prideful or have unrealistic beliefs about their abilities. I've actually had some people tell me, "Well, I don't want to build my kids' hopes up or paint a rosy picture for them or not be honest with them about life. My parents didn't speak a lot of positive things to me, and I didn't turn out that bad." This is not a healthy way to view things.

First of all, we should all want better input and output for our children than what we received. And secondly, we should realize that putting a positive spin on things whenever possible will go a long way to producing the behavior we desire to see in our children.

> Find ways to praise your kids and be a source of strength that nurtures their positive development. Positive words make your children shine brightly and reflect the goodness of God in their own unique way.

One of the things I teach at my karate school, our parenting boot camps, and our parenting coaching classes is the difference between *criticism* and *coaching*. For instance, let's say your child is running through the house screaming and yelling wildly. If you say, "Stop being so loud! You are driving me crazy!" – that's *criticism*. If you respond in this way, all he hears in his mind is, *I'm so loud. I drive her crazy.* That is not going to produce the positive change you're after. Instead, when your child runs through the house screaming wildly, you should say, "Hey, remember—walk and use your inside voice, please." In this way, he hears the command, "Walk and use my inside voice." That's *coaching.*

Criticism is always talking about the behavior you *don't* want. Coaching is seeding and telling them the behavior you *do* want. What you talk about is what you are going to get.

Your children will become what you say they are. If you repeatedly point out that they are stubborn, lazy, rebellious, or slow in school, that is what they will be. Instead, point out the positive things you see them doing, no matter how rare, and make a big deal out of it. Label them as great leaders, great readers, great friends to others, determined, disciplined, and every other godly quality you can find in Scripture. Encourage them with words like, "Wow, you did a good job cleaning your room, Johnny. I'm very proud of you! Make sure you check your chore chart so that you don't miss anything. I'll be back to see how you did later. You are becoming so responsible!" Or, "You worked so diligently in dance class today! I can really see you improving! That kick was awesome!" Praise pours positive power into the lives of our children, which we will see more clearly in the next chapter.

Realize that from time to time you may still want to say negative things. That's natural. Our flesh wants to get back at our kids for being difficult or embarrassing us. When this happens, say nothing about the behavior or issue until you are under control. Calmly tell them to go to their room and wait for you. This gives you time to cool off, pray and respond rather than react. If something negative should slip out, admit that you were unkind and apologize to your children, making sure they know that you love them, accept them and believe that they can do better.

> Point out the positive things you see them doing, no matter how rare, and make a big deal out of it. Label them as great leaders, great readers, great friends to others, determined, disciplined, and every other godly quality you can find in Scripture.

## Become a Good Listener

Another very important quality to cultivate to help you harness the power of your words is being a good listener. Ecclesiastes 3:1, 7 (NLT) says, "For everything there is a season, a time for every activity under heaven. ...A time to be quiet and a time to speak." And James 1:19 (NIV) tells us, "...everyone should be quick to *listen*, slow to speak and slow to become angry." Boy, there is a lot to learn in these verses. First of all, as parents, we have to learn to *slow down*.

Stop for a minute and let that sink in. Slow down—don't be so busy that everything is one big blur. Take the time to actually look into the eyes of your children and listen to what's on their heart. Look away from the TV, computer, and cell phone, and put down the newspaper. How important do you feel when the person you are talking to doesn't even look at you? Eye contact is critical when listening to your kids.

Secondly, being a good listener means learning when *not to talk*. I know this can be hard—especially for those of you who, like me, have been "wired from birth" to speak. Nevertheless, it can be done. The fact that God gave each of us *one* mouth and *two* ears tells us that we need to listen twice as much as we talk. Being quiet and attentive to what your kids are saying communicates that you value and respect them as a person. By giving your kids respect, you can expect to receive respect from them. Teach them how to tell you how they feel calmly and respectfully, without ugly words or harsh tones. This is a life skill that can be coached and developed. Ask questions to clarify that you understand what they are saying and to show that you care. Learning to really listen to your kids while they are young paves the way for heart to heart communication during the adolescent years.

> As a parent, you have to learn to *slow down*. Don't be so busy that everything is one big blur. Take the time to actually look into the eyes of your children and listen to what's on their heart.

## Keep the Lines of Communication Open

Keeping the lines of communication open between you and your children is extremely important. The power of your words is greatly diminished if this connection is damaged or broken. The best way to repair and maintain this vital link is to develop the habit of spending time with your kids. In other words, *build a relationship*. The stronger your relationship is, the more easily they will open up to you. And there will be less friction between you and them when you need to bring correction. All relationships need time and attention to grow—even the ones with your kids.

One of the greatest places you can connect with your kids is around the dinner table. There is just something about "breaking bread" together as a family and discussing the events of the day that knit you together in true unity. I encourage you to eat as many meals together as a family as you can. Some helpful hints to make the most of your mealtime include sitting together around the table, turning off the TV, and keeping the conversation upbeat. Mealtime is not the time to discuss major behavior issues or assign punishments. This can actually cause children to subconsciously associate eating with pain and cause them to develop digestive problems or even eating disorders. Yes, correct them if their manners are poor, but avoid dealing with deep issues.

You can also keep the lines of communication open by taking time to *play together*. As the old saying goes, "The family that plays together stays together." Take time to roll in the grass and throw a football outside. Tickle their toes and wrestle with them while sitting on the living room floor. Let laughter fill your house and love reign between you and your spouse.

Join in board games, read aloud, play hide-and-go-seek, and make memories that will last a lifetime. You only have a small window of time to invest in the greatest resource God has entrusted into your hands. Spend it wisely!

> The best way to repair and maintain the lines of communication between you and your kids is to develop the habit of spending time with them. In other words, build a relationship. The stronger your relationship is, the more easily they will open up to you.

## Learn to Speak Their Love Language

Each of your children (and your spouse) has a specific "love language." In other words, there is a specific way above all others through which they *know that they know* they are loved. Dr. Gary Chapman wrote a fantastic book covering this topic in great detail called *The Five Love Languages.* The five primary love languages are: acts of service, gifts, quality time, physical affection, and words of love and affirmation. Although everyone receives love though all these channels, and we need to express all of them to our children, each of us has a way that impacts us more than the others.

My daughter Shea absolutely loves getting gifts. I can buy her a $1 plastic dinosaur, and she thinks I'm the King of the World! Why? Because receiving gifts is her strongest love language. She also greatly appreciates when I spend quality one-on-one time with her. What do you think would happen if I only did acts of service to show her love? She would not feel the full extent of my love for her. Expressing your child's love language may require you to step out of your comfort zone. If you are not naturally affectionate or don't care about receiving gifts, you will have to step out of your "box" and deliberately and thoughtfully show your kids love in the way they can understand it.

One way to determine your children's primary love language is by paying attention to the way they express their love to you most often. If they wrap up their toys or make things and then give them to you, receiving gifts is probably one of their main love languages. If they enjoy doing things with you out in the yard, in the kitchen, or by your desk, spending quality time together is probably a major way they receive love. If they are always helping around the house, you can bet their love language is acts of service. The child who lavishes compliments on others would like to hear some as well, and the one who is always first in line for a hug needs more physical affection. Find out what each of your children's primary and secondary love languages are, and begin "speaking" them.

> The five primary love languages are: acts of service, gifts, quality time, physical affection, and words of love and affirmation. Find out what each of your children's primary and secondary love languages are and begin "speaking" them.

## Watch Your Nonverbal Expressions

The Bible says that "a *gentle* answer turns away wrath, but a harsh word stirs up anger" (Proverbs 15:1 NIV). I have learned that this verse not only applies to the words we speak but also our *tone of voice* and *nonverbal expressions,* also known as *body language.* Smiling at your kids or giving them the evil eye from across the room will work the same exact way as your words. Tension in your voice and on your face can make even soft words seem harsh.

I will go back to Shea, to give you a perfect example of this is principle. She is a wonderful child who has an amazing gift with language and an extraordinary imagination. However, she does have some learning challenges involving visual and auditory processing and attention deficits. When she was 5, she began visual processing therapy at a local clinic known for their excellence in working with these types of issues. After a few weeks, Shea began to tell us that she was stupid and was not doing well in her sessions. She revealed that the therapist was making "mean faces" at her and would not give her a reward sticker because she was not trying hard enough. I called the clinic to get their side of the story, and the therapist said that Shea was not focused on her tasks and kept looking at the therapists' face for confirmation that she was doing everything correctly. To discourage this, the therapist was keeping her face hard and tight. In my daughter's view, she was expressing disapproval. For Shea, it had the same effect as if the therapist had actually called her stupid.

My point here is: our nonverbal expressions are communicating a message beyond our words. If aggravation, irritation, anger, or rejection is written on the "headlines" of your face, your children will have a hard time believing and receiving any instruction you are trying to give them. If you are gritting your teeth, rolling your eyes, or throwing your hands in the air in despair while they are talking to you, you are not communicating a positive message.

What can you do when the pressure of the situation is mounting? Take two or three deep breaths (without sighing heavily) and if necessary, politely put the situation on hold. I am a big fan of the time tested tradition of sending your child to their room and simply telling them, "We will talk about this later." In the meantime, you will have some time to pray about the situation and even seek counsel from others if you need it. By the time you have to deal with your child, you will be in the right frame of mind to bring the appropriate correction and direction they need. The key is to *stay in control.*

> Our nonverbal expressions are communicating a message beyond our words. If you're gritting your teeth, rolling your eyes, or throwing your hands in the air in despair while they're talking to you, you're not communicating a positive message. The key is to stay in control.

## Learn to Say "I'm Sorry"

Now, you may be thinking, Okay, Mike. What if I mess up? What if I explode in anger or say the wrong thing or say something the wrong way? What am I supposed to do? The answer is, learn to say "I'm sorry." It's okay to apologize to your children. It's a healthy way to teach them humility and how to take responsibility for their actions. Just say, "I'm sorry. I should not have said that. I'm not perfect; God's still working on me. Will you please forgive me? Please pray that God will help me be the best mom/dad I can be for you." But don't stop there.

Once you apologize, speak some positive words of truth over your children to counteract the negativity. You can say something like, "I love you. You're precious to me. We're going to work on this together and find a solution." Send forth the power of life into your children and their situation, using positive words. A sincere, heartfelt apology can work wonders in your relationship with your kids.

Learn to say "I'm sorry." It's okay to apologize. It's a healthy way to teach your children humility and how to take responsibility for their actions.

## Start and End on a Good Note

What else can you do to effectively harness the power of your words? Start and end each day on a good note. As often as you can, wake them up in the morning with a warm, positive greeting like, "Hello, beautiful girl! Good morning, handsome boy! How's my super star today? How's my sweetheart? God's got great plans for you today!" It is truly amazing how positive words spoken first thing in the morning will help set the tone for the entire day.

And the same way you start the day is a great way to end it. Before you send your kids off to sleep, speak over them words of blessing, safety, and security. Lay your hands on them and pray for them, thanking God for all the good things that happened that day and blessing them with good dreams. Don't go over the laundry list of everything they did wrong. If you say things like, "Well, you didn't finish your homework tonight, so you can't go out and play tomorrow," or "No treats for you tomorrow because your room wasn't clean. And don't whine about it; you did it to yourself," what kind of sleep do you think they are going to get? It's not the right time to try and teach them a lesson. Instead, send them off to bed with words of love and affirmation dancing in their head. Get the lesson in the next day, when you can properly dissect what went wrong.

Speaking a warm, positive greeting in the morning and loving words of acceptance and blessing at night is a powerful thing you can do for your children. Try it for a week and watch the wonders it works!

> Start and end each day on a good note. Wake your kids up in the morning with a warm, positive greeting, and send them off to bed with words of love and affirmation dancing in their head.

## Get God Involved!

Now you can better see how your words define your kids. They contain the power to produce life or death in their lives. How can you get a better grip on the words that come out of your mouth? *Get God involved*. That's what King David did. He said, "Set a guard over my mouth, Lord; keep watch over the door of my lips" (Psalm 141:3 NIV). He also prayed, "May the words of my mouth and the meditation of my heart be pleasing to you, O LORD, my rock and my redeemer" (Psalm 19:14 NLT). Certainly, this is a timeless prayer we would all benefit from praying **every day**.

So pray and ask the Lord to place a guard over your mouth, stopping you before you say something mean or hurtful. Ask Him to help you *slow down* and become a good listener and watch your body language. He will reveal your children's love language and show you how to keep the lines of communication open and say "I'm sorry" when you need to. Keep in mind that if you weren't raised like this, it's going to take some time to harness the power of your words. But don't give up, God will give you the strength you need to do all things!" [3]

## TAKE AWAY

- WHAT ARE THE TOP 3 NUGGETS OF WISDOM YOU CAN TAKE AWAY FROM THIS CHAPTER?
- WHAT PRINCIPLES ARE YOU ALREADY DOING?
- WHICH ONES DO YOU NEED TO PRAY AND ASK GOD TO HELP YOU PUT INTO PRACTICE?

---

**PARENTING 101 RECAP**: Your words contain the power of life or death. They mold, shape, and *define* who your kids become. The behavior you see in them is, by and large, a harvest of what you have seeded over and over again with your words. With God's help, you can break any pattern of poor parenting, learn to choose your words wisely, and do what is necessary to harness the power of your words.

# Chapter 3

# *Employing the Power Of Praise*

"Don't use foul or abusive language. Let everything you say be good and helpful, so that your words will be an encouragement to those who hear them."

— Ephesians 4:29 NLT

Without question, words are powerful. The way we use them determines whether we are in the demolition business or the construction business. While negative, faultfinding words bring destruction, positive words of praise and encouragement build up and strengthen. In all my years of experience, one of the single most effective influences I have seen in a child's life is the *power of praise.* Nothing has a greater influence to motivate children in the right direction than encouraging words.

When our children are under the age of two, they hear words of praise and encouragement all day. Words like, "What a strong boy! Mommy's so proud!" seem to flow freely to kids at that stage of life. When they go potty, they hear, "What a big girl! You made poo-poo!" When they are learning to eat, parents say things like, "Oh, look at you. You've got food all over your face. You're so cute!" When they are learning to walk, they are encouraged with, "Come on, you can do it! You can make it! Walk to Daddy."

Then when children start getting into everything, between the ages of two and four, the amount of praise they receive drops in half to make room for correction. Suddenly they are hearing, "Don't touch that!" and "Don't run in the street!" about as often as they are hearing, "What a fast runner you are!" and "You're just the sweetest girl in the world!" They are still the apple of their parents' eye; the amount of praise they receive just diminishes.

During the elementary school years, corrections continue to rise from now both teachers and parents, criticism from peers begins in earnest, while affirmations continue to decrease. By the time they reach the preteen years of eleven and twelve, the amount of praise they receive declines to only two or three occurrences a day.

Finally, when the world is throwing sex, drugs, alcohol, and peer pressure at them in their teen years, they are lucky to receive one word of praise and encouragement a day. I believe this is why teenagers have so much trouble with rebellion, feelings of failure, and distrust. There's no blessing being spoken over them and into their lives. All they hear about is what they are doing wrong.

In all my years of experience, one of the single most effective influences I have seen in a child's life is the *power of praise*. Nothing has a greater influence to motivate children in the right direction than encouraging words.

Think about it. What would happen if we treated our teenagers and children of all ages like we treat our babies? What would happen if we showered them with praise and encouragement every day, saying things like, "You're awesome! You can do this! You're going to make it!" Does the parent of a child who is learning to walk and has fallen two, three or ten times say, "You stink; give up. You'll never walk." Of course not! That's when we encourage them all the more, and that encouragement lifts them over the hurdles of hardship and places them on the path to success. Without question, employing the power of praise produces positive results!

## Apply the "PCP Principle"

Bringing correction to our children is one of the chief responsibilities of every parent. By "sandwiching" discipline between words of praise, we can make it even more effective and actually encourage our children through it. This is called the "PCP Principle"—praise, correction, praise. It means you give your children praise, then correction, then praise again. Jesus Himself employs this principle when bringing correction to five of the seven churches in Revelation 2 and 3. It is a powerful model for parents, teachers, coaches, employers and spouses.

Take this common scenario as an example. "Jimmy" runs into the house with his report card. He has worked hard and has earned all A's and one C in math. What would most parents do? They would focus on the C saying, "Hey, what happened here? Why did you get a C in math? You didn't tell me you were having trouble. This really disappoints me." Jimmy would immediately be on the defensive and feel that his achievement of excellence in his other subjects was totally overlooked. Not only is this method unfair, it is also ineffective. When we apply the PCP Principle to this situation, Jimmy's parents' response would sound something like: "Wow! Look at all the A's you earned. You got an A in history, an A in science, an A in English, and an A in spelling. That's awesome! Hey buddy, what happened here with math? Do you need a little more study time with that or maybe a tutor? We can have a talk with your teacher and find out the best way to help you. I know you can bring this up, Jimmy. You've conquered C's before. You're smart, no doubt. We'll figure this out. We always team up—we never give up. Now let's go celebrate those A's!"

Notice the pattern—*praise, correction, praise*. This is so much more effective than just zeroing in on their weaknesses. Not only does it help our children overcome their difficulties, it also strengthens our relationships with them. Am I saying our kids have to be straight A students? No. The last thing we want to do as parents is put unrealistic expectations of success on our children. Not every child will achieve the same level of excellence in academics or sports or music. All we want to do is encourage them to do their best in whatever they are doing.

> The most effective way to bring correction is by "sandwiching" it between words of praise. It is called the "PCP Principle"—praise, correction, praise. It means you give your children praise, then correction, then praise again.

Are you having trouble getting your kids to clean their room or pick up after themselves? Try using the PCP Principle to motivate them. If you tell them to clean their room and then go in later and find the bed isn't made right, there are still a few toys out, and some dirty socks are on the floor, don't have a meltdown and start yelling about everything they didn't do. Instead, look for what they *did* do right and praise them for it. Any effort they put forth to obey should be praised. As long as they are moving forward in the right direction and improving, it's worth mentioning. You can say something like, "Wow, your bed is looking better and better. And most of your toys are put away. Way to go buddy! Oh, it looks like you missed a couple of things. How about remembering to put *every* piece of dirty clothes in the hamper, like these socks here? And don't forget to pick up your coloring books and check under the bed for toys. Other than that, you are really improving. I'm so proud of you! Finish doing these few things and go check what privilege you get for having your room clean."

The PCP Principle can be applied in virtually every area of instruction and correction. Realize that whatever you are trying to teach your children to do, it is going to take them time to learn. They probably won't "get it" or do it as well as you would like immediately, and that's okay. Ask God for grace—divine strength and ability—to talk to your children and correct them the way you yourself like to be talked to when you are in the process of learning something new. Aren't you glad that God is patient, kind; slow to anger, and forgiving when He corrects us?[1] Let us imitate Him, as His way is perfect.[2]

## Say What You Want to See

Another important point to realize is that people cannot process negative commands. They just don't understand them. If your child is acting up and you tell them to stop acting like a fool, in their mind they hear, *Act like a fool.* If you say, "Don't hit your sister," they hear, *Hit your sister.* If you say, "Don't be wild and obnoxious," they hear, *Be wild and obnoxious.* Try it for yourself. If I tell you, "Don't think about pink elephants," what does your mind begin to think about? Yep...pink elephants. The reason this happens is because we think in pictures about what is being said. That is the way our brain works.

We must learn to *say what we want to see.* We must speak the instruction that will produce the positive behavior we are looking for. For example, instead of saying, "Stop acting like a fool," you can say, "Straighten up. Act wisely." Likewise, instead of saying, "Don't hit your sister," or "Stop being wild and obnoxious," you can say, "Keep your hands to yourself. Be calm. Show me your best manners." In this way, you are communicating the positive behavior you want to see in a way their minds can understand it. This is what I call "seeding" the behavior you want. Our words are like seeds, so by planting the right seeds, we will harvest the right behavior.

We also need to avoid saying negative, destructive statements to our children. As I said in the previous chapter, negative, hurtful words spoken in anger are painful, and they have lingering and limiting effects on the future of your children. Instead of saying, "You are so stubborn," which is a negative, destructive statement, say something like, "You have the spirit of a leader, and you won't be easily misled." Again, it's all about putting a positive spin on the words of correction and instruction we are giving.

Learn to *say what you want to see.* Speak the instruction that will produce the positive behavior you are looking for. In this way, you are communicating the positive behavior you want to see in a way their minds can understand it.

# Pre-Frame Their Behavior

Seeding the conduct we want to see in our children is all about *pre-framing* their behavior. Pre-framing behavior is telling your kids *ahead of time* what you *want* and *expect* from them in a positive and affirming way. Once you tell them how you want them to act, you then follow it up with words of encouragement and praise, expressing to them that you know they can do it. Let's say you are going out to dinner and your kids have often cut up and made a scene when you went to a restaurant in the past. Begin to pre-frame the behavior you want and expect from them early in the day. Tell them, "Hey guys, we're going to Joe's Pizza Place tonight. When we go in, I want to see restaurant manners—napkin and hands in your lap and chew with your mouth closed. I want you to say please and thank you to the waiter and smile and look him in the eye when he is speaking to you. Sit still in your seat and respect everyone else in the restaurant by keeping your voices down. This is a special treat." Once your kids know what you want and expect, follow up your instruction with positive praise. Say something like, "I know you can do this. You're awesome! Show me how well you've learned your manners. I'm so proud of you."

Pre-framing behavior is not something we do every now and then—it is an ongoing method of training that helps our kids remember what is expected of them. Don't think your kids are going to hear instructions from you once or twice and remember them. More often than not, you are going to have to repeat the instructions again and again until the behavior becomes a part of their nature. The truth is we all need to be reminded of how to act. That is one of the greatest reasons God gave us the gift of His Holy Spirit after Jesus left the earth—to remind us of how Jesus taught us to live.[3] Repetition is the best teacher.

> Pre-framing behavior means telling your kids *ahead of time* what you *want* and *expect* from them in a positive and affirming way. Once you tell them how you want them to act, you then follow it up with words of encouragement and praise, expressing that you know they can do it.

So, pre-framing gives our children a clear understanding of what is expected of them and empowers them with words of praise to carry it out. In their minds, they hear, "This is what mom and dad want. And they believe that I can do it. I've got what it takes." Not only does this kind of training get our kids moving in the right direction, it also helps reduce our level of irritation and aggravation with them. Less irritation and aggravation means less stress and more peace—something all of us could benefit from.

At this point, you may be thinking, *but Mike, what if they don't listen? What if I pre-frame their behavior and empower them with praise and they still start fighting, screaming, or throwing food? What am I supposed to do?* That's a good question. Many parents have had this happen. If your kids have a track record of bad behavior in public, the best thing to do after you are sure they understand what is expected of them is to communicate what the consequences will be if they behave poorly. Say something like, "If you guys act up while we are in the restaurant, we are going to leave. We will go home and you will have peanut butter and jelly for dinner." Make the consequences clear and follow through if they behave poorly. Get up and leave the restaurant – get your food to go – and feed them peanut butter and jelly at home while you enjoy your take out. Trust me, they will not soon forget that lesson. We will cover the importance and power of following through in more detail in an upcoming chapter.

## Practical Ways of Employing Praise

What are some practical ways to employ the power of praise in the lives of your children? By speaking words of encouragement, creating a culture of love, identifying and nurturing their gifts, becoming a "good finder," creating a wall of victory, and making the most of every moment, you can communicate love and approval to your children.

## Create a Culture of Love

Having a quality relationship with your children is not about buying them a bunch of toys or giving them special privileges. A quality relationship is more about giving and receiving love. It is about nurturing your kids with hugs, words of praise and encouragement, and spending time together. This includes speaking those three powerful words to them again and again so they know they are valued—the words "I love you."

Neither my wife, Glori, nor I grew up in a family that said "I love you" very much. This is something we have consciously and deliberately changed in our home. We have created a culture of love. When all our kids lived at home, we told them we loved them every day. My oldest son in college plays linebacker on the football team. Even though he is bigger than me and a tough young man, he still hugs me and tells me he loves me on the phone and in front of his friends. Our other two kids in college get regular "I love you" texts. With my youngest daughter who is still at home, we say I love you to each other every time we come and go from the house and before going to bed.

> Having a quality relationship with your children is not about buying them a bunch of toys or giving them special privileges. It is about nurturing your kids with hugs, words of praise and encouragement, and spending time together.

Can you tell your kids you love them too much? Does it water it down? I don't think so. Saying *I love you* and *I'm proud of you* pours concrete into your relationship with them. It solidifies your connectivity. And as fathers, the tangible love that we show our kids gives them a vivid picture of how God loves them. Many people who have had difficult fathers don't believe in a loving God. Since their earthly fathers didn't say I love you or demonstrate their love, it is hard for them to comprehend the unconditional love of God. Love unexpressed is not felt by the other person. By saying I love you and coupling it with a hug or a gentle touch, you stay connected with your children.

I encourage you to hug and kiss your children whenever you have the opportunity, and take time to talk to them about your love for them. With a humble heart, ask them, "How do you know that I love you? What makes you feel loved and valued?" Listen to their response and take it to heart. Their answer will reveal their language of love. The more your kids *know that they know* you love them, the more impact your words will have and the more obedient they will become. As a result, your relationship will deepen and grow to new levels.

> Hug and kiss your children whenever you have the opportunity, and take the time to talk to them about your love for them. With a humble heart, ask them, "How do you know that I love you? What makes you feel loved and valued?" Listen for their response and take it to heart. Their answer will reveal their language of love.

# Be a Good Finder

Have you ever experienced a time in your life when all you could see in your child was their faults and failures? When their behavior irritated you so much that you didn't even want to be around them? This is a phenomenon that all parents go through at various times with each of their children. If this describes how you feel right now, you are on notice—Satan is at work. Revelation 12:10 says that he is the "accuser of the brethren," bringing our faults before God day and night. He is the one who is magnifying your child's mistakes and weaknesses in an attempt to divide and conquer. There is only one foolproof way to combat his evil tactics and that is by doing good.[4] In this case, it means becoming a "good finder."

You will find what you look for. The Bible says, "Whoever seeks good finds favor, but evil comes to one who searches for it."[5] If we look for everything our kids do wrong or leave undone, we will certainly find it. But if we look for what they do right, we will find that instead. It's the case of seeing the glass half empty or half full. It all comes down to the way you *choose* to see things. To be a good finder, you must purposely look for good things about your children and focus on them.

Being a good finder includes *thinking* about the good things our kids do, *talking* about the good things our kids do, and *writing* them down on paper. Meditate on and thank God for the good qualities he has put in your children, compliment your children when you catch them doing something right, talk to your spouse and parents about the cute and funny things they do, and write a "victory list' of their achievements over the last year. Philippians 4:8 says it best, "Summing it all up, friends, I'd say you'll do best by filling your minds and meditating on things true, noble, reputable, authentic, compelling, gracious—the best, not the worst; the beautiful, not the ugly; things to praise, not things to curse" (The Message). As you fix your mind and mouth on the good things in your children, being a good finder will become a habit. The more you do it, the easier and more effective it will become.

Being a good finder includes *thinking* about the good things your kids do, *talking* about the good things your kids do, and *writing* them down on paper. As you fix your mind and mouth on the good things in your children, being a good finder will become a habit.

## Identify and Nurture Their Gifts

Another powerful way to build up your children and pour praise into their lives is by helping them discover and develop their God-given gifts. Every one of us is born with a unique combination of talents and abilities. Scripture even goes so far as to say, "Each person is given something to do that shows who God is" (1 Corinthians 12:7 The Message). Sometimes our children's gifts are obvious, and other times they are not. As parents, it is our job to become a "talent scout" and help our kids find out what they are naturally good at and what they enjoy doing, and then train them up in their gifting.

You may be familiar with Proverbs 22:6, which says, "Train up a child in the way he should go, and when he is old he will not depart from it" (NKJV). The Amplified Bible adds a whole new dimension to this verse declaring, "Train up a child in the way he should go [and **in keeping with his individual gift or bent**], and when he is old he will not depart from it." By helping your children discover their God-given gifts and who He made them to be, you show them you value them as individuals and the purpose that God has for their life. Whatever they are interested in, whether it is art, music, athletics or academics; sign them up for lessons or clinics, check out books at the library about the subject and people who achieved greatness in that field; rent inspirational movies to motivate them to improve; and coach them on the importance of regular practice. Become their biggest fan and cheerleader.

You need to encourage and praise your kids in their abilities— even if you have no personal interest in what they are good at doing. I have seen a family of athletes look down upon their academically inclined son because they could not understand why he would rather read about insects than play football. You must allow God to define and refine who your children are, not your personal preferences. Never compare them to yourself or their siblings. Support them completely in their endeavors and their confidence and self-esteem will soar.

> You need to encourage and praise your children in their abilities—even if what they like has no interest to you. You must allow God to define and refine who your children are, not your personal preferences.

## Create a Wall of Victory

Creating a "Wall of Victory" is another great way to employ the power of praise. It reminds your children of their past successes and helps motivate them when facing new challenges. Select a wall in their bedroom or the family room and put up a bulletin board to display your children's achievements. Include certificates and ribbons for placement and participation in spelling bees, team sports, special contests, church events, etc. Post report cards filled with good grades. Put up pictures of activities they were a part of, such as helping at a community cleanup, serving at a soup kitchen or retirement home, or assisting at a school function. Be creative. Anything you can include to celebrate their successes will make a great addition to this wall of victory—even if it's something they did for fun, like run in a school race or help out at Vacation Bible School. The objective is to *build a success bank account* in their mind.

The Wall of Victory gives your children a resource to remind them that they are capable of doing big things. When they are striving for a goal and the going gets tough, bring them to the Wall and talk about the situations and achievements represented there. Recalling memories of great efforts that led to success builds confidence. While most people review their past failures in times of challenge, you can teach your children to review their past triumphs and watch them overcome any difficulty!

## Make the Most of Every Moment

Life flies by at an amazing speed. We often think things will slow down just as soon as we finish this project at work or as soon as the holidays are over. But there is always new busyness to replace the old busyness. The next thing you know, your children are off to college and careers and your relationship with them changes, never to be the same again. To truly connect with our children and our spouse, we must learn to choose our outside-the-family commitments wisely and seize the family opportunities set before us. I know firsthand how challenging this can be. Like you, I am worn-out at the end of the day and come home and want to just plop down on the sofa to read and relax. But the truth is, the time we have with our children is very limited, and we must make the most of every moment.

What if you knew you had just one minute, a mere sixty seconds, each day to talk to your kids. What would you say? What would you share with them and speak into their lives to fill them with courage and confidence and set their life in the right direction? What would you *not* say? What words and phrases would you eliminate from your conversation altogether? Let's take it one step further. What if you found out you were dying and this was the last time you had a chance to say something to your children. What would you tell them? What would you impart to them about who they are in Christ, based on the truth of God's Word and the love in your heart?

Ask yourself those questions everyday and speak the words they need to hear now before the time of your influence with them runs out. This is why God tells us, "Look carefully then how you walk! *Live purposefully* and worthily and accurately, not as the unwise and witless, but as wise (sensible, intelligent people), *making the very most of the time* [buying up each opportunity], because the days are evil. Therefore do not be vague and thoughtless and foolish, but understanding and firmly grasping what the will of the Lord is" (Ephesians 5:15-17 AMP).

I encourage you to live each day as if it were your last—not in fear but in faith and with a strong sense of purpose. Our parenting years are also the career and home-building years—the time when we have personal God-given dreams of our own that we long to fulfill. In His wisdom, God has entrusted us with many assignments in this season of life. He will never ask us to do something that He will not enable us to do. So, get up every morning and surrender your dreams to God knowing that your relationship with your spouse and children is what matters most in this life. When your priorities line up with God's priorities for your life, He will enable you to achieve more than you ever thought possible.

> What if you knew you had just one minute, a mere sixty seconds, each day to talk to your kids. What would you say? What would you share with them and speak into their lives to fill them with courage and confidence and set their life in the right direction? Make the most of every moment.

# Speak Hope and Blessings

As a karate instructor, I regularly encourage my students. I tell them how great they are, that they are going to be awesome future black-belt leaders, and that they can make the honor roll in school that year. I say, "This is the year you are going to learn how to ride your bike...play the trumpet...make the team..." etc. Whatever they are working on, I tell them they can do it. Interestingly, many parents seem uneasy about me saying these things to their kids. When I ask them why, they usually say, "Well, I just don't want them to get their hopes up." This kind of thinking is debilitating and goes against God's Word. It weakens our kids and hinders them from reaching their full potential. We all need hope. Hope is critically important to a person's success and happiness.

God is all about hope. As a matter of fact, He is called the *God of hope.*[6] In talking about our future, Jeremiah 29:11(GW) says, "I know the plans that I have for you, declares the Lord. They are plans for peace and not disaster, plans to give you a future filled with **hope.**" Therefore, if God wants us to believe there is a hope-filled future ahead for us, He wants our kids to believe there is a hope-filled future ahead for them. He wants us to cast a vision of a big, bright future for them.

Many children grow up without hearing word of hope from their parents, as I did. The absence of verbal approval and affirmation, especially from my father, definitely limited my capacity to succeed for many years. Then one day several years ago, I felt impressed by the Holy Spirit to contact my dad about this issue. While I was praying, I heard in my heart, "Michael, you need your dad's blessing." Out of obedience to the Lord, I e-mailed my father and asked him point- blank, "Dad, can you tell me a specific time and a specific thing I did in my life that you were proud of?" As far as I could remember, he had never told me he was proud of me.

Hope is critically important to a person's success and happiness. God is all about hope. As a matter of fact, He is called the *God of hope*. He wants us to cast a vision of a big, bright future for them.

Well, he ignored the question completely. All he talked about was the weather and the stock market—all the surface stuff that he and so many others like to talk about to avoid deeper issues. But I wouldn't let it go. Again, I asked the question, "Can you tell me a specific time and a specific thing I did in my life that you were proud of?" At that time, I was about forty-one years old, parenting four kids, and operating my own business and I still desperately wanted my father to bless me with his words.

A few weeks passed, and we had gone around and around this question. Finally, my dad responded to what I asked. In an e-mail, he said, "How about every day of your whole life?"

I was stunned by his response. "Why didn't you ever tell me?" I asked.

"I was afraid it would make you soft," he answered.

Although my dad's words were late and few, they have made a positive impact on my life since then. It is never too late for your words of encouragement to deeply impact your kids.

The power of *life* is in your tongue, and God wants you to use it to bring life to your children. He says, "...Let everything you say be good and helpful, so that your words will be an encouragement to those who hear them" (Ephesians 4:29 NLT). This doesn't mean you pretend they have no flaws or never discipline them for rebellion or disrespect. We will cover discipline in-depth in the next chapter. It just means you choose your words wisely, remembering that the ultimate goal of your parenting is to raise strong, godly kids who make an impact society.

> The power of *life* is in your tongue, and God wants you to use it to bring life to your children. The ultimate goal of your parenting is to raise strong, godly kids who make an impact on society.

## What's a Proven Recipe for Effective Praise?

For your praise to be effective, you must follow a few simple guidelines. Always be sincere and always be specific – kids can smell a fake a mile away. Consider saying, "Great job on cleaning your room, I like the way you arranged you stuffed animals so neatly!" Praise your child's efforts more than his abilities. Say, "I am so proud of you that you learned to tie your shoes. You never gave up, even when the going got tough. Your diligence and perseverance paid off!" Focus on your child's personal achievements, the things that make them special, and avoid comparing your kids with each other or anyone else. Say "You danced so beautifully in the recital! I spotted you right away by your great posture!" Smile, make eye contact, and get down on your knees so that you can talk with them on their level.

Use words of praise and encouragement to effectively bring correction to your kids. Use them to seed and pre-frame the good, godly behavior you want to see. Use them to create a bright future and build big dreams. Don't withhold praise and blessing from them. If there are any personal obstacles hindering you from speaking words of encouragement to your kids, pray and ask the Lord to help you identify and overcome them. By His grace, you can become a good finder, learning to focus on the good in them.

Your children are eagerly waiting to hear that you are proud of them. Like a thirsty man in the desert heat, they long for your love, acceptance, and encouragement. Give them what they need and long for. Build their self-esteem and confidence. As you learn to employ the language of praise and approval, your words will become a powerful force to shape the lives of your children.

**TAKE AWAY**

- WHAT ARE THE TOP 3 NUGGETS OF WISDOM YOU CAN TAKE AWAY FROM THIS CHAPTER?
- WHAT PRINCIPLES ARE YOU ALREADY DOING?
- WHICH ONES DO YOU NEED TO PRAY AND ASK GOD TO HELP YOU PUT INTO PRACTICE?

---

**PARENTING 101 RECAP**: Employing the power of praise is an effective way to positively impact and motivate your children. By using the PCP Principle, *saying what you want to see*, and pre-framing their behavior, you can more successfully bring correction to your kids' conduct. Practical ways of employing the power of praise include creating a wall of victory, identifying and nurturing their gifts, becoming a good finder, and creating a culture of love. Start applying these proven principles with your children, and watch the difference it makes!

# Chapter 4

# *Creating Change Through Consequences and Consistency*

"Discipline your children while there is hope. Otherwise you will ruin their lives."

—Proverbs 19:18 NLT

I have had the privilege of meeting and working with thousands of parents at my karate school and through parenting conferences and coaching sessions. The most frequently asked question I get is: "Mike, how can I get my kids to *change their behavior*?" The answer is simple – through consistent discipline. Although this is an old-school line of thinking, it still holds a proven track record of success.

We don't have a crime problem in the U.S. We have a punishment problem.

People caught breaking the law often plea bargain their way out of punishment. They either avoid jail completely or they go and get out in a matter of months. In the same way, you don't have a behavior problem in your house – you have a follow through, or enforcement, problem. Discipline inconsistency applied, and failure to enforce consequences, leads to rebellion.

Your kids are destined by God to do great things. But in order for their destiny to become a reality, they need the priceless gift of discipline – and you are the primary instrument God has commissioned to administer it. It has been said before, and I will say it again: Discipline is the divine link between desire and destiny.

> How can you get your kids to *change their behavior*? The answer is simple—through consistent discipline. Your kids are destined by God to do great things. But in order for their destiny to become a reality, they need the priceless gift of discipline.

## What Is Discipline?

The root of the word discipline means *to teach*, to disciple. When we discipline, we instruct the minds of our kids, preparing them to live in a godly way by teaching them correct principles and habits. Yes, discipline includes administrating consequences, but the thrust of it is teaching. When consequences are needed, they should have a teaching element attached for them to work with maximum impact. And all discipline must be done calmly.

So you may be asking, "Mike, what's the difference between consequences and punishment?" We discipline out of love; we punish out of anger. Enforcing consequences designed to teach in a relaxed, businesslike manner is correct and Spirit-led. Yelling, getting angry, and wanting to get back at your kids for their behavior is punishment, which is of the flesh. Jesus said, "It is the Spirit Who gives life [He is the Life-giver]; the *flesh conveys no benefit whatever* [there is no profit in it]..." (John 6:63 AMP).

Colossians 3:21 says that as fathers we are not to *embitter* our children. The Amplified Bible really spells out what this means, saying, "Fathers, do not provoke or irritate or fret your children [do not be hard on them or harass them], lest they become discouraged and sullen and morose and feel inferior and frustrated. [Do not break their spirit.]" While we need to discipline our kids, we must be careful not to be so hard on them that we break their spirit. God helps us maintain this balance through our relationship with Him. He helps us keep the main objective of parenting before us at all times—building a healthy, whole person.

Since discipline is essentially teaching, we are bringing discipline to our kids all the time. Some of the best teaching moments I have found are when our children are in an upbeat, positive state of mind. This may be when you are coming home from a restaurant or movie, spending time together at the beach or around the pool, or playing games at the kitchen table. Seize those moments to speak into their lives. Let's say you are driving home from the movies, and there was something in the film that connects with a behavior you have been working on with one or more of your children. That can be a teachable moment. By teaching them while they are in a peak emotional state, the truth of your words can deeply penetrate their heart.

When is the best time to bring correction for improper behavior? The *first* time it happens. The moment you recognize wrong attitudes and actions, prune them – nip them in the bud. The problem in many people's homes is they think their kids' behavior patterns just grew from nothing, like a phantom vapor. The truth is, our kids are regularly testing the boundaries of our tolerance with their behavior, seeing what they can get away with. When they are not corrected for their improper behavior, they will continue in that behavior. The opposite of that is just as powerful. When *consequences* are carried out, children will *not* continue in that behavior since it does not benefit them to do so.

The word discipline means *to teach*, to disciple. When you discipline, you instruct the minds of your kids, preparing them to live in a godly way by teaching them correct principles and habits. Some of the best teaching moments I have found are when our children are in an upbeat, positive state of mind. In this peak emotional state, the truth of your words can deeply penetrate their heart.

## Consequences Are Critical

"When the sentence for a crime is not quickly carried out, the hearts of the people are filled with schemes to do wrong" (Ecclesiastes 8:11 NIV). No scripture more clearly communicates the need for swift consequences better than this one. People continue in behaviors that have no consequences attached to them. If your children are constantly getting away with doing things that are wrong, what is their motivation to change?

Our children's actions require specific responses – both for acceptable and unacceptable behavior. While praise and rewards should be given for obedience and initiative, which we will tackle in detail in the next chapter, removal of privileges and correction should be implemented for disobedience and irresponsibility. In each situation, the punishment should always fit the crime. In other words, take away a privilege that corresponds with what they did wrong.

I have found that the best way to connect an appropriate consequence with inappropriate behavior is to Decide In Advance (DIA). If you are married, sit down with your spouse and talk and pray about the best course of action to take. If you are a single parent, take time to carefully and prayerfully consider what to do. Decide In Advance which consequences should be given for specific inappropriate behavior.

Once you decide on the consequences, clearly communicate them to your children. Warn them that if the unacceptable behavior continues, they will face the consequences. Say the problem you are dealing with is that your child won't get up in the morning on time. Inform them, "Starting tomorrow you must get up cheerfully the first time I ask, or you will have to go to bed right after bath without playtime so that you can get more sleep." You may have to do this for days before the behavior you are wanting kicks in, but don't get discouraged. Be persistent and consistent. Consistency creates credibility; credibility creates compliance (obedience).

By the way, a lecture is *not* a consequence. One time a dad told me his two sons, ages six and seven, had broken two or three rules of their home. So he sat them down and talked to them for twenty minutes about what they did wrong. I asked him, "Did you take away their video games for the weekend? Did you take away their bikes? Did you tell them they couldn't go outside and play with their friends?"

"No, but I gave them a good talking to," he said.

Again, a "tongue lashing" or a lecture is NOT a consequence. A consequence is the removal of a privilege. Taking away something that our kids really enjoy gets their attention. Yelling at them doesn't work. The moment we start yelling, our teaching stops and they mentally tune us out. They just don't hear what we are saying. Calmly removing a privilege, on the other hand, speaks volumes.

> Our children's actions require specific responses—both for acceptable and unacceptable behavior. While praise and rewards should be given for obedience and initiative, removal of privileges and correction should be implemented for disobedience and irresponsibility.

What privileges can you remove? Watching television is a privilege. Playing video games, surfing the Internet, hanging out with friends, and having dessert are privileges too. For teenagers, having a cell phone is a coveted privilege they don't want to lose. Other privileges include driving, playing on a sports team, going shopping, going on vacation, and attending summer camp. Really, the only rights your children have are to a roof over their heads and meals. Just about everything else is a privilege. This fact has been forgotten by many families today.

I suggest you make a list of all the things your kids enjoy doing. These are all privileges that should be tied to good behavior. Attach them to the conduct that you are trying to instill in them or correct. Tell them, "If you do 'this' (insert desired behavior), you can have 'this' (insert privilege they enjoy)." This makes them take ownership of their actions.

You can also use privileges as motivation for being responsible around the house. This teaches them, when they are young, the importance and value of contributing to the family. For example, you can say, "You may play outside when your bed is made and the dishwasher is emptied." This will also teach them the critically important life lesson of "work first, play second." Once your kids know what you expect of them and the consequences that they will face if they don't obey, you must follow through with what you said you would do.

> Make a list of all the things your kids enjoy doing. These are all privileges that should be tied to good behavior. Attach them to the conduct that you are trying to instill in them or correct. You can also use privileges as motivation for being responsible around the house. This teaches them the importance and value of contributing to the family when they are young.

## Whatever You Do, You Must Follow Through

Practical consequences that are consistently enforced create boundaries that effectively deter kids from unacceptable behavior. For example, if your child's grades don't match their potential, suspend use of all electronics so that they have more time to study. Cancel play dates and sleepovers so that they can focus completely on their school work. Of course, help them or get a tutor if needed. When the first few test grades come in improved, you can gradually restore them to full privileges.

The consequence your child needs may not be the easiest thing for you to carry out, but whatever you say you'll do, you must follow through. If you say "If you do X, then Y is going to happen", make sure that "Y" happens! Otherwise your children will lose their trust in and respect for you and even their feelings of security. At that point, their behavior may even get worse as they try to push you to set the limits they need to feel safe and loved.

> Consequences that are consistently enforced create boundaries that effectively deter kids from unacceptable behavior. The consequence your child needs may not be the easiest thing for you to carry out, but whatever you do, you must follow through.

Like most parents who have teenagers, we too have had to deal with getting our kids to abide by the rules. One of the biggest we have had to enforce is the curfew we set. At our house, the consequence for breaking curfew is you lose your driving privileges for a week.

My oldest son, Austin, saved his money for years to buy a car. The August before his junior year, with a little help from our gift matching what he had saved, he chose a safe, reliable vehicle. Life was good.

Then Austin went out one Saturday night and broke his curfew. He came home about thirty minutes late, and I was waiting for him. As he walked in the door, I said, "What's up, son? What time's curfew?"

He said, "Eleven. Oh, but Dad, there were a lot of red lights, you know. And I got a little lost coming home."

In a calm and controlled way I said, "Let me have your keys."

"What do you mean?" he stammered. "I was lost. I got caught by all the lights. And I...."

"Well, you also didn't give yourself enough time to get home," I responded. We have a saying at our house: *Better to be thirty minutes early than one minute late.* Punctuality is one of the keys to showing respect and responsibility.

So I took my son's keys away, and he lost his car and driving privileges for a week. That meant he couldn't drive the following weekend – the weekend of the homecoming dance at his high school. Now, missing curfew didn't mean he couldn't go to homecoming, because the predetermined consequence attached to coming in late was losing his driving privileges for the week.

Much to Austin's dismay and despite the fact that I had a friend in town, I drove him and his date to the homecoming dance. I didn't deliberately embarrass him in front of his friends, or add any extra humiliation to the consequences. I simply and calmly took the car away, although it meant I would be inconvenienced by having to drive him myself. It was essential that I follow through even though it was the first time he was late. He needed to know that I meant business.

Austin did not break curfew again for many months. He did come home late another time after that, and again he lost his driving privileges for a week. He was testing the boundaries as many teenagers do, just to be sure that I still meant what I said. When he saw that I did, he went back to following the house rules and was never late again.

Make a list of all the things your kids enjoy doing. These are all privileges that should be tied to good behavior. Attach them to the conduct that you are trying to instill in them or correct. You can also use privileges as motivation for being responsible around the house. This teaches them the importance and value of contributing to the family when they are young.

## Let Them Feel the Pain

Over the years, I have had dozens of grandparents bring their grandchildren to our karate school. After they had been with us for awhile and I had established a trusting relationship with them, I asked them, "Why are you bringing your grandkids to karate? Where are their parents?" In most cases, I would hear that their parents were in prison, they had skipped town, or they were dead from a drug overdose.

In light of their answers, I then respectfully asked them, "If you could turn back the clock and go back to when your children were kids, what would you do differently – what would you change so that there might have been a different outcome?" With tears in their eyes, almost every grandparent answered, "I didn't let them feel the consequences of their actions. I made excuses for them; I cut them slack, and I wish I hadn't. I knew the teacher/principal/judge/cop, and I got them out of trouble over and over again." By deflecting the consequences that would have come from their children's actions, the parents did them a grave disservice. Their kids never learned the consequences of wrong choices when their troubles were a tiny sapling, and as a result their troubles grew into great oak trees they could no longer uproot.

Not too long ago I was talking to a friend whose teenaged son had started smoking. He asked me what he should do to get him to quit. My response: "Take his car away."

"I can't do that," he responded.

Time passed and the man's son started drinking. He was eventually pulled over by the police and given a ticket for speeding. Instead of letting his son feel the pain of his consequences, he paid for the ticket. Again, he asked me, "What should I do? Now he's drinking. How do I handle this?"

"Take his car away and sell it," I answered.

"Oh, I can't do that." He replied. "He needs it to get to work."

"Well, you can bring him back and forth to work," I said. But he would not heed my counsel. Later, I heard that his son got expelled from his college housing for smoking pot. Now the kid is living back at home, parading his rebellious example in front of his younger brothers and sisters.

As a parent, you can learn a valuable lesson from the pain of others. Train your children when they are little. Let them feel the consequences of their inappropriate behavior. Let them make an F in school and have to go to summer school to retake a class because they goofed off during the year. Let them get kicked off the football team or do community service because they got caught with alcohol. As hard as these consequences may seem, they may be just the thing your son or daughter needs to keep them from going off the deep end later in life.

You can cushion your kids' consequences with kindness and compassion. You should hug them, love them, and pray with them that God will help them through it. But don't take away the consequences. They must feel the pain of the poor choices they make when the consequences are safe and small. Consequences should be smart, swift, and real. In this way, not only do they train the one they are given to, but also his brothers and/or sisters. Remember, "Poverty and shame come to him who refuses instruction and correction, but he who heeds reproof is honored" (Proverbs 13:18 AMP).

> As a parent, you can learn a valuable lesson from the pain of others. Train your children when they are little. Let them feel the consequences of their inappropriate behavior. As hard as these consequences may seem, they may be just the thing your son or daughter needs to keep them from going off the deep end later in life.

## Stay Calm, Cool & Collected

Along with Deciding In Advance (DIA) on the appropriate consequences for your children's inappropriate behavior and following through, it is also very important to correct them with the right attitude. You must stay calm, cool and collected. When yelling starts, rapport is broken and teaching stops. If you explode in anger or frustration, your kids are going to deflect part of the responsibility for their behavior onto you. They will say things such as, "Dad's mean." "Mom yelled at me." "They don't love me." They know just what to say to shift the focus off of what they did and onto how you responded. That is why you have to remain in control and act businesslike when you discipline.

Staying calm, cool and collected also helps you avoid giving out consequences that are too harsh or not enforceable. Have your kids ever done something that really ticked you off, and then you flew off the handle and told them, "You're grounded for a year!" or "You can't go to your friend's house ever again!" The problem with consequences issued in anger is that we usually have to abandon them after coming to our emotional senses.

A better way to handle a highly heated situation is to immediately send your child to his room. Take a deep breath, relax, and calm yourself. Talk to God about it and if you are married, get your spouse's input. If you need to, call a godly friend. You don't have to have all the answers immediately. Give yourself a break. Once your emotions settle down, you can DIA the best consequence for your child's inappropriate behavior. When you are calm, you are ready to talk to them. You know what the consequence is going to be and are able to clearly communicate it to them.

Another valuable tool I recommend parents use is open-ended consequences. This is excellent for kids that are ten and up, especially teens. An open-ended consequence is one that is enforced until your child's behavior *improves.*

By their behavior choices, they get to decide when they regain the privileges they lost. Simply say, "This is not open for discussion or negotiation."

Make sure that you let a reasonable amount of time pass before you declare them restored. Reformed behavior should be seen for a least a week, but go as long as the offence requires. I once removed cell phone privileges from one of my sons for nine months, until I felt he had fully overcome his behavior issue.

I have seen many kids who had a specified length to their consequence have a really bad attitude toward their parents for the duration. They take the stance, *Okay, so I'm grounded from TV and my cell phone for a week. No big deal. I'll get it back next Monday. I'll make my parents miserable in the meantime.* In a situation like this, an open-ended consequence forces the child to take personal accountability for his actions *and* keep a good attitude toward you. When the behavior and attitudes improve to your satisfaction, restore privileges.

I'm not big on giving a lot of warnings. For example, when it's time for my kids to clean their rooms, I usually incorporate the warning with the instruction. I say something like, "Hey, I'm coming back to check your room in fifteen minutes, and it needs to be clean. When it is, you can go outside." I outline what I expect, I remind them of the privilege that is attached to the job, and I encourage them to get it done. If I come back and the room is not clean, they lose their chance to go outside and they still have to clean their room.

You should never do the ever popular "count to three" technique. Children should be taught to stop inappropriate behavior the first time you ask. Counting to three actually trains them that it's OK to keep on doing what they shouldn't be doing until you get to three. "What a fun game to watch Mommy and Daddy get madder and madder as they count! As long as I stop before three, nothing happens to me!" Looking at it from the child's point of view, you can see it's just not a productive form of discipline.

It is important to realize that there is a great opportunity for strife to enter your relationships with your children while administering consequences. Satan will do his best to take advantage of the situation and drive a wedge of anger and resentment between you and them. As the parent, you can't allow this to happen. Pray and ask God for strength to love them and stay connected. Hate the rebellious, inappropriate behavior, but not your children. You are not wrestling against flesh and blood. It is a spiritual war that will be won spiritually.[1] During this time, make sure you draw close to your children. Don't give them the cold shoulder, even though you may want to. Spend time talking with them and give them extra hugs. Choose the Spirit over the flesh.

Remember, don't embitter your kids. Temper everything you do with wisdom and love. As God's Word says, "...Be quick to listen, slow to speak and slow to become angry, because *human anger does not produce the righteousness that God desires*" (James 1:19,20 NIV).

Don't let your emotions take the lead in your discipline. Give it in a calm, cool and considerate manner.

> It is very important to correct your kids with the right attitude. This means staying calm, cool, and collected. When yelling starts, rapport is broken and teaching stops. Temper everything you do with wisdom and love, not emotions.

## Be Consistent

Another key component to successful discipline is being *consistent*. Without consistency you have chaos and your kids never know what to expect. Being consistent means the standards of right and wrong in your home don't change and they are continually enforced. Your kids know the behavior you expect from them. It is *firmly fixed* in their minds. They know the rules and the consequences of breaking them. They also know the rewards for obedience and the privileges that come with doing what is right.

The more consistent you are in your discipline, the more your kids are going to automatically know what you expect. For instance, if my daughter says something rude or breaks a specific house rule, she automatically knows the consequence. There have been times when she has said, "Oh oh, that's it. I lost my treat this week, didn't I?" She was right. She knew the consequence because she had been taught. For her, removing treats is definitely effective. It's a consequence I suggest you try in your own home.

One of the best ways to help create consistency in your discipline and your children's behavior is by posting the "house rules." These are the universal, "one size fits all" guidelines that apply to all of your kids. Make a list of the top ten rules you want them to learn and obey and attach a scripture to as many of them as you can. These should be printed out and posted in a prominent place, such as near the kitchen table, in the living room, or in their bedrooms. Next to the house rules, post a list of the privileges they enjoy. By posting the rules and the privileges that come with them, they will know what you expect and be motivated to obey.

Once the house rules are on display, it's important to review them on a regular basis. We should never assume our children are automatically going to remember them just because we told them once or twice. Everybody needs to be reminded of what is expected of them, especially children. Think about it. I have employees that have been with me for years, who occasionally still forget a step in a procedure they have completed fifty times before. How often does a newlywed wife have to remind her husband to please put the toilet seat down? It takes time to learn new habits.

Consistent discipline with consistent consequences works. Being consistent in your discipline empowers you to identify and deal with wrong attitudes and behaviors right when they start. By catching things early, you can avoid the forming of bad behavior patterns or habits that are much more difficult to break once they are established. Consistently applied discipline with consistent consequences brings consistent, positive results.

Being consistent means the standards of right and wrong in your home don't change and they are continually enforced. One of the best ways to help create consistency in your discipline and your kids' behavior is by posting the "house rules." By posting the rules and the privileges that come with them, they will know what you expect and be motivated to obey.

## What About Spanking?

Up to this point, all of the consequences for inappropriate behavior that we have talked about have dealt with removing privileges. There is another consequence that cannot be overlooked and that is spanking or "administering the rod." I know that this is a very sensitive subject in our culture—even among many Christians. Therefore, I am going to share what the Bible has to say about it as well as some personal experiences.

When I was growing up, I was spanked. Actually, it was really more of a smack with a wooden spoon, or some pretty strong hits with a belt. Although I don't think of myself as abused, I would definitely never suggest giving out this type of correction. Yes, it did help me avoid a few specific behaviors, but there is a better way. What kids need is loving correction aimed at softening their rebellious will but not hurting their tender spirit.

What does God have to say about spanking? Everyone has heard "spare the rod, spoil the child," but that's not what God's word says. "He who spares his rod [of discipline] hates his son, but he who loves him disciplines diligently and punishes him early" (Proverbs 13:24 AMP). That means that if we spare the rod, we show that we don't love our kids the way we should. Proverbs 29:15 (NIV) goes on to say, "the rod of correction imparts wisdom, but a child left to himself disgraces his mother." And Proverbs 22:15 (NASB) tells us that "Foolishness is bound up in the heart of a child; the rod of discipline will remove it far from him." So according to these scriptures and others, spanking should be a part of our discipline, and we should implement it when our children are young—between the ages of two and twelve. It should always be done in love, not anger, and in control, not out of control.

In my opinion, children should only be spanked for *willful or repetitive disobedience* and *disrespect* or *dishonor* of parents. They should understand that your God-given job as mommy/daddy requires you to correct their poor behavior. Let's say your child is in the first grade and you tell him to do his homework. Defiantly, he replies, "No, I'm not going to do it!" Immediately and with firmness, you should say, "This is the last time I'm going to tell you. Sit down and do your homework or we are going to go to your room and you're going to get a spanking." If he listens and obeys, nothing need be done. If he disobeys, follow through with the spanking.

Here is another example. Let's say you are teaching your son that calling mommy a "stupid head" when she doesn't give him what he wants is disrespectful and contrary to God's will for his behavior. The first time it happens, you instruct him not to do it. The next time he says it, you take away a privilege as a consequence and give him additional instruction. You calmly inform him that if he disrespects his mother again, he will face the consequences of the rod of correction. The very next time he does it and from that point on, administer the rod. If you allow disrespect or disobedience to become a habit when your children are little, it will mushroom into bigger problems that are harder to break when they are older. Depending on how far you have allowed the poor behavior to go, it may take several spankings to bring about the right behavior.

Your kids should know that when you get very calm and say, "Go to your room. I'll be there in a few minutes," they can expect a spanking. At this point, they may try to negotiate, saying things like, "How many am I going to get? How about just one? Can it be a soft one?" If they do this, just turn and say, "Go to your room. You know what we expect from you. You mustn't disrespect your mother and me that way." A few minutes later, you should calmly go to their room and give them two to four swats on each cheek of their behind. The number of swats should be determined by the severity of their disobedience or disrespect and the strength of the will of the child. Whatever the number administered, it needs to bring them to repentance—the softening of their will to submit to your teaching.

After spanking them, pray with them. Ask God to give them the ability to hear, obey and respect your instruction. Remind them that we all fall short and make mistakes[2] and that only through the power of Jesus Christ can any of us be obedient to our parents and to God. Let them ask God for forgiveness. Reassure them that God loves them and forgives them and that you do too. Let them know they are growing in their obedience, self-discipline, and ability to be respectful. Give them a hug and with that, your relationship is reestablished, and positive results will be produced.

Now, you may be thinking, *Mike, how do I know how hard of a swat do I give them? I don't want to hit them too hard.* That's a good question. To see how strong your swat feels and how much force you should exert, make sure you give yourself a swat first. Remember that kids are smaller and do not require as much pressure as you do. And, *Should I use my hand or a ruler?* Hands are for loving, so I suggest a wooden or rubber ruler.

I also want to say that when you first begin to spank your kids, you will probably feel bad about it because of a past worldly view of spanking or because you have memories of being spanked in an inappropriate way. If you do, pray and ask God for strength to work through it and press in. In time, you will feel more comfortable with spanking your children when their behavior warrants it, especially when you see the results that come from doing it God's way.

According to the scriptures, spanking should be a part of our discipline, and we should implement it when our children are young. They should only be spanked for *willful or repetitive disobedience* and *disrespect* or *dishonor* of parents. It should always be done in love, not anger, and in control, not out of control.

Please, don't misunderstand me. I do *not* believe in child abuse in any form. I think that slapping a kid in the face or hitting them across the back of the legs is not only wrong but ineffective. Slapping a child on the knuckles with a ruler is also unacceptable. We can also throw out methods like making children kneel in the corner on rice or corn, standing outside in the heat, or spanking them in public. But we can't throw out the baby with the bathwater. God says there is redeeming value in spanking our kids. Yes, maybe we were spanked too hard or too often for the slightest offense by our parents when we were little. Perhaps they were red-faced, screaming and out of control. But we shouldn't throw out spanking altogether. Using an appropriate-sized rod or ruler isn't going to hurt them—it's going to help them.

The bottom line is: "Don't be afraid to correct your young ones; a spanking won't kill them. A good spanking, in fact, might save them from something worse than death" (Proverbs 23:13,14 The Message). Pray and ask God to show you the best way to handle spanking in your home. He will help you decide what is best for each of your children.

## Paint Them a Picture

I'll never forget a conversation I had with my son when he was in his senior year of high school. He was an honor roll student, a football player, a responsible, hard worker, and had a scholarship to college. It was just before his prom, and he came to me and said, "Dad, I want to go to the prom on the party bus with some of the football team." Here's where I had to help him see what could happen. Teens and kids usually can't see several steps ahead in a decision making process.

"Okay," I said. "You are responsible enough now that Mom and I will let you make this decision. But let's talk about what it looks like." So I asked a few questions. "Will there be drinking on the bus?"

He said, "I guess so."

"Do you think you can resist the temptation when it is all around you?" I asked.

"I guess so," he replied.

"What happens if you have a drink?" I questioned.

"You sell my car," he replied. He knew the consequence because we had talked about frequently.

I then asked, "What does that look like to you?"

"Well, you put a for sale sign on my car," he answered.

To that I said, "No, not exactly. It looks like this. I take the car to a used car lot and get rid of it. When you wake up the next morning, the car will be gone. Sold. After I take out my investment, I will give you back whatever is remaining. You can use that money to buy another used car, but I will not help you financially. You will be totally on your own. Whatever you find, you buy."

"Wow...really?" he responded.

"Yes," I said. "And you'll have to pay for all of your car insurance. I will not pay for half of it anymore. Which means you can't afford to drive anymore. That's what it looks like, son. So sleep on it. Think about it. Can you really tell your date and your friends and the driver, 'Hey, stop this bus. There's alcohol on it, and I've got to get off. I'm not going to get in trouble with you guys.'"

He woke up the next morning and came to me and said, "Dad, I'm not going on the party bus. I'll be home after the prom."

"Why did you decide that?" I asked.

He replied, "It's just not worth the risk."

Wow! What a wonderful moment in a parent's life.

Kids, especially teenagers, can't always connect the dots to see what the outcome of their actions will be, so you have to paint them a picture. Sit down and walk them through the possible consequences of the choice they are thinking about making. You want them to be able to see that the principles you are teaching them and the rules and consequences you have in place are boundaries that keep them safe—just like God's Word creates boundaries that keep us safe when we obey it.

Discipline is an expression of love, not hate. God delights in the son He disciplines. He disciplines us because He loves us. "No discipline is enjoyable while it is happening—it's painful! But afterward there will be a peaceful harvest of right living for those who are trained in this way" (Hebrews 12:11 NLT).

If you love your kids you'll discipline them. It is what sets them on the path to success.

Discipline is an expression of love, not hate. God delights in the son He disciplines. He disciplines us because He loves us. And if you love your kids you'll discipline them too. It is what sets them on the path of success.

## Our Ultimate Goal

Remember, our goal with discipline is to teach. Our aim is to see the outward discipline we have imparted to our children become self-discipline and self-control that guides and protects them for the rest of their lives. Through consistent discipline with consistent consequences, you can bring positive change to the lives of your children.

It's your responsibility as a parent to teach your children. If you don't teach them, the teachers will. If the teachers don't teach them, the principal will. If the principal doesn't teach them, the school board will. If the school board doesn't teach them, the police will. If the police don't teach them, the judge will. If the judge doesn't teach them, the penitentiary will. If the penitentiary doesn't teach them, the grave will. Don't let it come to that. Discipline weighs ounces; regrets weigh tons.

If you are feeling regret for falling short in your God-ordained role as disciplinarian to your children, ask God to forgive you and give you the strength to change. Invite Him into every area of your life. Apart from Him you can do nothing, but through Him, you can do all things![3] He will help you become the parent your kids need to grow up and experience the wonderful life He has planned for them. He has the incredible ability to turn the mess we have made of our lives into a miracle worth celebrating.

## TAKE AWAY

- WHAT ARE THE TOP 3 NUGGETS OF WISDOM YOU CAN TAKE AWAY FROM THIS CHAPTER?
- WHAT PRINCIPLES ARE YOU ALREADY DOING?
- WHICH ONES DO YOU NEED TO PRAY AND ASK GOD TO HELP YOU PUT INTO PRACTICE?

---

**PARENTING 101 RECAP**: The way to change your children's behavior is through consistent discipline. Discipline means teaching your kids to live God's way. Practical consequences and consistency are vital to good discipline. While praise and rewards should be given for obedience and initiative, removal of privileges and correction should be implemented for disobedience and irresponsibility. Consequences that are consistently enforced create boundaries that effectively deter kids from unacceptable behavior.

# Chapter 5

# *Motivating Your Kids In Key Areas*

"Let us think of ways to motivate one another to acts of love and good works."

— Hebrews 10:24 NLT

How can you motivate your kids to reach their God given potential? This is a critically important question – one that truly needs thought, prayer and continuing attention.

Can you stimulate, inspire, and spur them in the right direction without being a nag? Sure, you can! The foundation for motivating your kids is a solid relationship between you and them, which is second only to helping them develop a personal relationship with God. These relationships are like the bookends in their lives. They provide stability, strength, and structure for their growing spirit, soul, and body.

In this chapter, we will look at both *how* and *where* to motivate your children. Along with building your relationship with them and connecting them to God, we will examine how you can help them stay focused, establish routines, and develop a thankful heart. Some key areas we will zero in on include doing chores, eating healthy, and getting along with siblings. Let's see how all these elements work together.

> The foundation for motivating your kids is a solid relationship between you and them, which is second only to helping them develop a personal relationship with God. These relationships are like the bookends in their lives. They provide stability, strength, and structure for their growing spirit, soul, and body.

## Build a Good Relationship

Having a good environment in your home is essential to raising your children and motivating them to make positive, healthy choices. The center of that environment is the quality of the relationship you share. If your kids feel loved, they are going to listen to you. If they feel valued and appreciated, they are going to want to please you and do what you ask. If they don't feel loved or valued, they will eventually rebel.

As Josh McDowell powerfully put it, "Rules without relationship lead to rebellion." Having a connected relationship with your kids is the indispensable key to motivating them.

How do you see your children? Are they an aggravation you tolerate? Or are they a blessing from God? Psalm 127:3-5, in The Message Bible, gives us God's view of our kids. It says, "Don't you see that children are God's best gift? The fruit of the womb his generous legacy? Like a warrior's fistful of arrows are the children of a vigorous youth. Oh, how blessed are you parents, with your quivers full of children! Your enemies don't stand a chance against you; you'll sweep them right off your doorstep."

Wow! Our children are a treasure. They are little people God has entrusted to us for a brief period of time to mold and shape and aim as arrows into the future. They need our love and acceptance.

The best way to express love and value to your kids is by spending time with them. Although the phrase *quality time* is overused, it's still important. It's the stuff memories are made of. Holiday traditions, summer vacations, and special family nights knit our hearts together like nothing else. For example, growing up in New Jersey, I was never much of a hunter or fisherman. However, while raising my sons in Louisiana, hunting and fishing became important to them – so I made it important to me. I only hunt when one or both of my sons go with me. When people invite me to go hunting or fishing, I ask them if I can bring my sons. I am trying to make the most of every opportunity to spend time with them and keep our relationship alive.

> "Don't you see that children are God's best gift? The fruit of the womb his generous legacy? Like a warrior's fistful of arrows are the children of a vigorous youth. Oh, how blessed are you parents, with your quivers full of children!"
>
> **—Psalm 127:3,4 The Message**

The *quantity* of time we spend together is also important. The more you are around your children simply "doing life" together, the more loved and valued they are going to feel. The more loved and valued they feel, the closer the connection will be between you and them. The closer you are connected, the more you will be able to influence and motivate them in the right direction. They will also be more inclined to open up and share their heart with you and more teachable moments will occur.

Use words of praise and encouragement to inspire them and infuse them with confidence. When you recognize their good qualities, they will want to please you more, and be more open to your coaching. Take time to listen to what they are saying. Talk about topics that are important to them. Again, this communicates that they are valuable and loved. I think every parent should read Dale Carnegie's book *How to Win Friends and Influence People* and apply the principles to their relationships with their kids. This classic how-to manual will show you practical ways to improve any relationship you have.

So, spend time with your kids. Find ways to connect and build your relationship with them. Make any necessary changes in your home and in your schedule to create a more loving and peaceful environment. Take time each evening to plan for the following day so it's less hectic. Make lunches, take baths, pick out clothes, etc. The less strife and chaos you have in your home, the more connected you are going to feel as a family and the more you are going to be able to influence your children to make right choices. You may say, "But Mike, we are so busy with 'X, Y, and Z' that we don't have time to spend together." My answer to you is that you must do whatever is necessary to make time for your kids, including changing jobs, downsizing your home –

whatever it takes. You only get once chance to raise your kids. Don't let it get away from you because you are too busy.

> The *quantity* of time you spend with your children is also important. The more you are with them simply "doing life" together, the more loved and valued they are going to feel. The more loved and valued they feel, the closer the connection will be between you and them.

## Teach Them to Be Thankful

Being thankful is the "mother" of all virtues and one of the most important qualities we must help our kids develop. Thankfulness should not be something we express just once a year on the fourth Thursday in November. An attitude of gratitude has a positive effect on every area of our lives. Think about it. A child that is grateful is also kind and generous. A child that is grateful is also peaceful and patient. Just about every good characteristic you want your children to have grows out of a thankful heart.

God knows the power and importance of maintaining an attitude of gratitude. That is why He says, "Be thankful in all circumstances, for this is

God's will for you who belong to Christ Jesus" (1 Thessalonians 5:18 NLT). No, we don't have to be thankful *for* all circumstances. We have to be thankful *in* all circumstances. This means looking for and focusing on things we can be thankful for. It's all about perspective. If your kids start complaining about not having the newest pair of tennis shoes, make them aware of children who are less fortunate than they are. When they realize that there are some kids who don't have a place to live or know where their next meal is coming from, they will see their situation in a whole new light.

I think one of the greatest things we can do is take our kids on a mission trip once they are old enough to contribute. When they see how children in other countries live and how little they have, their lives will be forever impacted. With a new perspective, murmuring and complaining will dissipate and give way to thankfulness in their hearts.

My wife and I have our kids go through their clothes and toys at least once a year and donate items that are clean and in good shape to organizations that help people in need. I know many families that give away their old clothes, furniture, and electronics rather than sell them at a garage sale. When they get a new TV, they give the old one to their church, where it is used as a tool to minister to children and youth. Out of a thankful heart, multiple seeds of love and kindness are sown. Through it all, children develop an attitude of gratitude, generosity, and selflessness.

> Being thankful is the "mother" of all virtues and one of the most important qualities we must help our kids learn. God tells us to be thankful *in* all circumstances. This means looking for and focusing on things we can be thankful for. It's all about perspective.

What else can you do to cultivate a thankful heart? Every night while putting your children to bed, count your blessings. Thank God for the things you have. Say, "Thank You, Lord, for Your protection and provision; for our food and clean water, the roof over our heads, our friends and family, and our health. Thank You for a job, our dog and cat, our parents, and our grandparents. Thank You for the birds, the sky, the mountains, the seas, and the trees. Lord, You are so great! Thank You for all the wonderful things You've done for us. In Jesus' name, Amen." Then ask your children what they are thankful for. When they see and hear your grateful heart, it will be contagious. Your example goes a long way.

If your children are complaining or being ungrateful, they need an attitude adjustment in their heart. The first thing we can do when our kids are being ungrateful is ask, "Aren't you thankful for..." and then remind them of good things God has blessed them with. The next thing we can do is quote 1 Thessalonians 5:18, and ask them, "Are you obeying God and being thankful in your circumstances?" This is why being in the Word and developing their love for the Lord is so important. Without that relationship with God, they don't care if they are obedient to Him. And if they don't know the Word, they won't know what God has to say about their behavior.

Lastly, we can have our kids write out a list of their blessings and put it on their Wall of Victory so that they can see it every day.

Take time to teach them that **everything** good they have is a gift from God.[1] This includes not only their material possessions, but also the air they breathe and their gifts and talents. Their ability to sing, play a musical instrument, hit a baseball, paint a picture, be kind and generous to others, and every other blessing comes from God. Teach them how to write thank you notes to those who have blessed their lives and to say please and thank you more often.

> When your kids see and hear your grateful heart, it will be contagious. Your example goes a long way. They need to be taught to be thankful for everything they receive.

## Establish a Routine

Another key factor to help motivate your kids and keep them on track is *establishing routines.* A routine is any action we do automatically on a regular basis. It includes specific duties and responsibilities that help children grow up to be self-disciplined. Routines can be established for everyday activities, household chores, as well as family fun times and devotions. They help children feel safe and teach them healthy habits, such as brushing their teeth, washing their hands, and taking a bath. Another wonderful aspect of routines is that they help eliminate stress and bring a tremendous amount of peace and order to the home because everyone knows what is expected of them. If established correctly, these set schedules can be a tremendous blessing to the entire family.

We are all creatures of habit. So much so that we will unconsciously create a routine if we don't already have one. For instance, there are some adults I know who were raised with watching television as a part of their daily routine. The first thing their parents did when they got up in the morning was turn on the TV. As a result, they have continued the habit in their own homes without even considering whether it is good for their family. Television has become a major distraction for them and their kids.

If the TV is on in the morning at your house, I suggest you pull the plug on it. Watching TV first thing in the morning gets children started off on the wrong track. It causes them to lose their focus on the tasks of getting ready for the day. Wake your children up with some words of encouragement, and tell them to begin getting ready for the day. Establish a set routine for them to go through before leaving the house for school. For example, have them get dressed, fix their hair, brush their teeth, wash their face, and make their bed. Instead of letting them watch a half hour of cartoons, start them off with a good breakfast and a few verses of scripture or a brief devotional. In the event that they are done with all their morning chores and have eaten breakfast and it's not time for school yet, they can play with their toys.

> A *routine* is any action children do automatically on a regular basis. They can be established for everyday activities, household chores, and family fun times and devotions. Routines help children feel safe and teach them healthy habits, such as brushing their teeth, washing their hands, and taking a bath.

The other critical time of the day for kids to have a set routine is before bedtime. They need to be in bed at the same time every night within a fifteen to thirty minute window. This helps set their circadian rhythm, or "body clock," to instinctively know when it's time to go to sleep. By getting up Monday through Sunday within thirty minutes of the same time, their body becomes internally regulated. Their immune system, musculoskeletal system, and brain function will all improve with a regular bedtime and rise time. Even better, a routine bedtime is one of the greatest ways to get your kids to fall asleep without a fight.

So after dinner, let them play a little while, give them a bath and read them a story. If you have multiple children, have everyone gather in the same room to listen together. When story time is over, pray a prayer of blessing over them. You will be amazed how much security and love this simple act instills in your kids. When you lay your hand on their head and pray for them to have good dreams and be protected through the night, you connect with their hearts in a powerful way. After prayer time, it's lights out.

Establishing routines like these develops discipline, and discipline connects your kids with their destiny.

> By getting up Monday through Sunday within thirty minutes of the same time, your children's body will become internally regulated. Their immune system, musculoskeletal system, and brain function will all improve on a regular bedtime and rise time.

## Help Them Focus

Once you have established a routine, it is much easier to help your kids stay focused and get things done. Another big secret to helping your kids focus is to *eliminate distractions.* Something I hear from parents time and again is, "My kid doesn't listen." The truth is, kids don't just magically listen. They must be *trained* to listen. This reminds me of a situation one of the families that attended our "Parenting Boot Camp" shared with us awhile back. The mother said, "My daughter just can't seem to stay focused on her schoolwork; she's always distracted. What can I do to help her?"

I began asking her some key questions. First, I asked her to tell me about her daughter's schedule. It really wasn't too bad, but it did reveal a couple of things. She was watching too much TV, which definitely hinders a child's ability to focus. She was also doing her homework after dinner, which is rather late in the day. The best time to do homework is right after school when the day's learning is still fresh in kids' minds.

Next, I asked her to describe her daughter's bedroom. This was the real eye-opener. Her room, as I suspected, was filled with numerous sources of distraction. Nowadays, kids' bedrooms are little kingdoms. They often have a TV with a DVD player, video games, computer, and a stereo, not to mention a cell phone. It's no wonder they can't focus on schoolwork when there are so many other more interesting things to do! When I pointed this out to both the mom and dad, they realized that what they had allowed their daughter to have in her room was the problem that led to her inability to focus on homework. Consequently, they removed all the recreational electronics and her grades immediately went up.

I have hundreds of stories like this, including situations in which children with cell phones were talking or texting at all hours of the night. Once the phones were taken away, their grades went up. I'll say it again, to motivate your kids to stay focused, you must eliminate distractions. Limit the amount of time they spend watching TV and playing video games; keep these activities in the den where they should be. Make their bedroom a place for sleeping, reading and resting. These guidelines, along with establishing good routines, will keep them focused and help them concentrate and perform better in school and all other areas of life.

> To motivate your kids to stay focused, you must eliminate distractions. Limit the amount of time they spend watching TV and playing video games. Be careful not to make their bedroom a place that is filled with distractions. Make it a place where they want to sleep, read, and rest.

## Overcome the Challenge of Doing Chores

One of the top three subjects I am asked about is how to motivate kids to do chores around the house. People say, "How do I get my kids to make their bed, do the dishes, fold the clothes, and run the vacuum cleaner?" First, make a chore chart of the things you want them to do and post it in their bedroom and in the kitchen. Put their *morning* chores on one page and their *evening* chores on another. These chores would include their routine before going to school and their routine before going to bed. A third page should contain a list of chores they are to do on a *weekly* basis. Make sure that you have taught them how to do each item on the list and they are confident in the skill.

Each chore on the list should be age-appropriate. You should not expect your five-year-old to wash their sheets or clean the tub, but you can expect your twelve-year-old to do it. For your little children, begin by letting them do things they can do for themselves. For instance, they can pull up their comforter over their bed and put their dirty clothes in the basket where they belong. As they grow, they will be able to begin dressing themselves and putting on their own shoes. Simply lay out their clothes the night before and in the morning tell them to get dressed. Say, "You know the routine. Get dressed, wash your face, brush your teeth, brush your hair, make your bed, and put your night clothes away. If any of your clothes are dirty, put them in the basket. Check your chore chart to make sure you remembered everything, and then come to breakfast." Realize that if you keep doing things for them that they can do on their own, they will have no motivation to learn how to do it themselves.

As your kids grow and mature, increase their level of responsibility. Add new items to their list, like taking out the garbage, straightening up the bathroom, vacuuming and dusting, doing the dishes, doing the laundry, and mowing the lawn. Some chores can be scheduled as a family activity, such as cleaning the garage and the attic and sprucing up the gardens for spring.

> Make a chore chart of the things you want your kids to do and post it in their bedroom and in the kitchen. Put their *morning* chores on one page and their *evening* chores on another. A third page should contain a list of chores they are to do on a *weekly* basis.

If you have small children, I encourage you to take pictures of their clean room and post them on the wall near their chore chart. You can also take pictures of any other room that you want them to clean. This will help them know what clean means to you and reduce the number of "do-overs" when expectations are not met. All directions should be clear and easy to understand.

If you do not give your children the responsibility of helping out around the house, they will develop an entitlement mentality. This means they will expect things to be given to them for nothing. They will feel you owe them something simply for existing. They must learn that they are expected to be a contributing member of the family, not a leech being served by others. Do not rob your kids of the satisfaction that comes from getting a job done and doing it with a good attitude.

By teaching your children to do their chores, you are preparing them for adulthood. Chores instill discipline, order, and a sense of responsibility in their lives. They give kids training for the real world and a feeling of accomplishment. So post their chore charts and make them simple and clear. Include a list of privileges they get for successfully completing each task. Don't forget to go over their chores and rewards with them on a regular basis, reminding them of the consequences for failing to complete them. Putting these things into practice will be a win-win situation for you and your kids.

Next to your children's chore chart, include a list of privileges they get for successfully completing each task. Don't forget to go over their chores and rewards with them on a regular basis, reminding them of the consequences for failing to complete them.

## Motivate Them with Rewards

Rewards are powerful motivators. If you have trouble getting your kids to do their chores, tie a specific privilege to the chore you want them to do. Let's say it's Saturday and they are ready to play outside but they have not completed the duties on their morning daily chore chart. Tell them calmly, "Once you have done all your morning chores you may go outside. Let me know when you are done and I will check your effort." Always follow up and make sure everything was done correctly and that they did not do a "rush job" in order to get outside faster. You will be amazed at how well things get done using this technique.

Reward your kids for *approximations of success*. Don't discourage them by expecting perfection right out of the gate. New skills take time to learn. Think about it. How do the people at Sea World find killer whales that can jump twenty feet in the air? Do they charter a huge seafaring ship, look for whales that are jumping twenty feet out of the water, and catch them? No. They catch a whale and then *train* it to jump. They start by putting a pole in the water and encouraging the whale to swim over it. When he does, he is rewarded with a bucket of fish. The trainers then move the pole up higher and encourage the whale to swim over it again. When he does, another bucket of fish is given to him as a reward. Again and again, the trainers raise the bar higher, rewarding the whale with fish every time he successfully makes the jump. Before you know it, he is jumping twenty feet. For your kids, set the bar at a reasonable height when they are learning a new skill. Reward them incrementally as they improve, but don't wait until they get it perfect.

> Rewards are powerful motivators. If you have trouble getting your kids to do their chores, tie a specific privilege to the chore you want them to do. As you coach them with their chores, *be specific*. Tell them exactly what you want them to do.

The first time my kids cut the lawn, it looked like someone chewed it up and spit it out. But I kept coaching them on how to do it, using the PCP principle. I told them, "Much better this week, you remembered to fill the mower with gas before you started! Next time, after three runs, empty the grass catcher. You are really getting good at this!" Each time they did it and they did a better job, I rewarded them with extra pay.

Don't think you are robbing your kids of their childhood by having them do chores. And don't think you are manipulating them by rewarding them for a job well done. All of us are motivated by the rewards set before us. The reward of a paycheck at the end of the week is what motivates most people to get out of bed every day and go to work. Even Jesus was motivated by the reward set before Him. The Bible says. "...He, for the joy [of obtaining the prize] that was set before Him, endured the cross, despising and ignoring the shame, and is now seated at the right hand of the throne of God" (Hebrews 12:2 AMP).

So, find the button that excites your kids and push it—reward them with the privileges that motivate them to get the job done.

> Reward your children for their approximations of success. With each step of improvement they show, praise and reward them in some way. Find the button that excites your kids and push it—reward them with the privileges that motivate them to get the job done.

# Educate Them on Eating

Motivating kids to eat healthy is the next item on our menu, and it is vitally important. Obesity in our country has now reached epidemic proportions—even among children. The diseases that often come with obesity—diabetes, heart disease, and stroke—are also on the rise. In many cases, these diseases are preventable by making some simple lifestyle changes, such as buying and eating healthier foods and increasing our amount of exercise.

The *New England Journal of Medicine (March 2005)* reported that this generation of kids – approximate ages two to fifteen – will have a shorter life span than their parents. This is the first reduction in life expectancy in over two centuries. The reason is because of sedentary lifestyle and nutrition that leads to obesity, type 2 diabetes, and many more lifestyle diseases.

This may sound strong, but I believe that feeding our children poorly is a form of child abuse. Young children do not get to decide what they eat. They have no control over what's in the pantry or the fridge, or what restaurants they are taken to. We, as their parents, are the ones who will be held accountable by God for how we trained our children to eat.

The first step to getting your kids to eat healthy is to just stop buying foods that are not good for them—especially "kid-friendly" foods. They are loaded with preservatives, artificial colors, and sugars. Refined white sugar and high fructose corn syrup are often the first or second ingredient in many foods marketed to children. Fake sugars, like saccharine and aspartame are sometimes thrown into the mix to make foods appear to be a "healthier" alternative, but they are actually worse due to their chemical content. Excess sugars, additives, and preservatives can be the culprit in attention issues in children. In my karate school, when parents eliminated high sugar foods from their diet, we saw great improvements in the behavior and attention span of some of our students with ADD and ADHD.

The first step to getting your kids to eat healthy is to stop buying foods that are not good for them—especially "kid-friendly" food. Excess sugars, additives, and preservatives can be the culprit in attention issues in children.

Now you may be thinking, *Wow! What am I going to give my kids to eat if I cut out all those kinds of foods?* Relax! Kids will learn to eat whatever you put in front of them. And as they develop a taste for real, whole foods they will eat a wider variety of them. If they are already junk food junkies, introduce healthy foods to them a little at a time. There is a healthier alternative for every junk food they eat. For example, exchange that inferior instant oatmeal that comes in the small brown pouches for the real deal you cook on the stove. You can add your own honey, cinnamon and blueberries or bananas. Next, try plain potato and tortilla chips instead of orange colored, cheese-flavored chips. Gradually reduce and then completely eliminate soda from your home. Your children should be drinking filtered water more than anything else.

Start them off when they are young with plenty of fresh vegetables. For optimum health, organically grown, raw vegetables should make up the bulk of your diet. Cut up carrots, celery, and broccoli and have them ready to snack on. Add a little raw spinach to a homemade fruit smoothie. Vegetables should be a part of every meal.

If you are having a tough time getting your kids to eat their veggies, keep trying different ones until you find a few that they can tolerate. Tell them "Eat your veggies first and then I'll serve you some mashed potatoes (or some other food that they like)." Or, you can tie it to a privilege, like playtime, video games, or a movie.

Once vegetables are a regular part of their diet, offer them fresh fruits. Slice up apples and oranges and have bananas, grapes and berries on hand. Fruit is naturally sweet and delicious and a viable alternative to prepackaged, high-sugar snacks.

Indulge in desserts only a few days a week. If you and your family are daily dessert eaters, call for a "sugar fast" in your home and see if you can all go for a week without sweets. Then, start back with just two or three treats a week. Some healthy desserts to try include strawberries with real whipped cream or baked bananas sprinkled with cinnamon and pecans.

Kids will learn to eat whatever you put in front of them. Begin introducing healthier alternatives to them a little at a time. There is a healthy alternative for every junk food they eat. Start them off when they are young with plenty of fresh vegetables. Once vegetables are introduced, offer them fruit.

What else can you do to motivate your kids to eat healthy? Take them to the supermarket and teach them how to look for fresh foods that are full of color and life. Let them pick and choose new foods to taste. As they get older, educate them on how food companies market their foods and spend millions of dollars creating a taste that hooks people into buying their product. You can also watch the movies "Food, Inc." or "Super Size Me," and if that doesn't scare you into eating right, nothing will.

Teach your children moderation in all of their food choices. Their health, attitude, ability to concentrate, and quality of sleep will improve when they're eating better. As you eat healthy along with them, you will reap the benefits as well.

> What else can you do to motivate your kids to eat healthy? Take them to the supermarket and show them how to look for fresh foods that are full of color and life. Let them pick and choose new foods to taste. Teach them moderation in all of their food choices.

## Promote Peace

Sibling rivalry is a problem in many families, but this is nothing new. Brothers and sisters have been fighting with each other since the days of Cain and Abel. The key to promoting loving sibling relationships is to teach your children to be kind and forgiving—to follow the Golden Rule and be a peacemaker. God says, "As much as it is possible, live in peace with everyone" (Romans 12:18 GW).

Our two sons fought frequently when Glori and I first married. One son came from my first marriage, and the other son came from hers. Add to this the fact that they are only about a year apart and have completely different personalities, and we had a recipe for major challenges. Tempers flared and competition thrived. We learned that the best thing to do when they fought was to give them open-ended consequences. We told them, "We will not tolerate this bickering and fighting. Neither of you can leave the house *until further notice.* We will restore your privileges when your behavior towards each other improves." With this, they were highly motivated to work together to develop their relationship and have freedom restored.

We taught our sons the importance of forgiveness and being kind. God says, "Be *kind* to one another, tender-hearted, *forgiving each other*, just as God in Christ also has forgiven you" (Ephesians 4:32 NASB). Everyone needs forgiveness because everyone makes mistakes. In order to *receive* forgiveness from God, we must be willing to *give* forgiveness to others. Jesus said if we don't give it, we won't get it.[2] If we will ask Him, He will give us the ability to both forgive and be kind, and this is what we taught our kids.

We also taught them the Golden Rule: "Do to others whatever you would like them to do to you. This is the essence of all that is taught in the law and the prophets" (Matthew 7:12 NLT). These words from Jesus, though they are over 2,000 years old, still apply to our relationships today—to those inside and outside our home. It never ceases to amaze me how people will treat total strangers better than their own spouse and children. I have seen people hold a door open for someone they don't even know, yet they wouldn't hold it open for their own wife or mother. I have watched others bump into a total stranger in the store and politely say, "Excuse me." Yet when they bump into their children, they say, "Get out of my way. Why don't you watch where you're going!" This should not be the case.

> Everyone needs forgiveness because everyone makes mistakes. In order to *receive* forgiveness from God, we must be willing to *give* forgiveness to others. Jesus said if we don't give it, we won't get it. If we will ask Him, He will give us the ability to both forgive and be kind.

The Scripture says, "...every time we get the chance, let us work for the benefit of all, starting with the *people closest to us* in the community of faith" (Galatians 6:10 The Message). We should be treating our family better than we treat total strangers. Our children should be treating their siblings better than they treat their friends. They are the ones that are closest to them and will be with them for their entire lives.

Living together peacefully is not something your kids will put into practice overnight. It will take consistent discipline that includes both teaching and consequences. If your kids continue to fight and argue with each other after you have corrected them, give them an open-ended consequence that best connects with what they were arguing about. Tell them, "Well guys, since you can't seem to share the television without fighting, you've lost your TV privilege. It is suspended until you can agree on a plan that works this issue out." Instruct them on how to sincerely apologize and then forgive each other. Coach them on how to resolve conflicts by being willing to compromise. These problem solving skills are critical to their success in future relationships.

Today our sons are good and loyal friends to each other. "How wonderful, how beautiful, when brothers and sisters get along! ...Yes, that's where God commands the blessing, ordains eternal life" (Psalm 133:1, 3 The Message).

> Instruct your kids on how to sincerely apologize and then forgive each other. Coach them on how to resolve conflicts by being willing to compromise. These problem solving skills are critical to their success in future relationships.

## Connect Your Kids with God

Out of all the things we have discussed, there is one duty as a parent that trumps them all. Connecting your kids with God is the most important job you have. By introducing them to the love of their heavenly Father and helping them build a relationship with Him, you set them up for success like nothing else can.

The Bible says that Jesus is the exact likeness of God the Father[3] and He loves children. Regardless of how many people were pulling on Him and vying for His attention, He still made time to be with kids. "One day children were brought to Jesus in the hope that he would lay hands on them and pray over them. The disciples shooed them off. But Jesus intervened: 'Let the children alone, don't prevent them from coming to me. God's kingdom is made up of people like these.' After laying hands on them, he left" (Matthew 19:13-

15 The Message). Just as God longs to be in relationship with adults, He longs to be in relationship with children. Age is not a boundary for Him. Samuel, David, and Timothy are all examples of God's desire to connect with our kids.

> Connecting your kids with God is the most important job you have. By introducing them to the love of their heavenly Father and helping them build a relationship with Him, you set them up for success like nothing else can.

When children know that they are truly loved by God and understand who He is and what He has done for them, they desire to be pleasing to Him just as we do. Our job is to instill God's Word in their hearts and cultivate their love for Him so that the Holy Spirit can do His sanctifying work. Read the Bible aloud at the dinner table or at story time and discuss how it applies to their daily life. Implement a scripture memory program with rewards for each new scripture they learn. Speak scripture over their lives.

Use daily devotional books written especially for kids to teach them how to read God's Word on their own and pray about what they read. Teach them to listen for His still, small voice. Talk to them about His goodness and about your relationship with Him. Show them how they can live to glorify God.

God's abiding presence stays with your children forever. He will show them the best choice to make in every situation as they stay connected with Him. As they grow to love Him with all their heart, soul, mind and strength nothing will be able to motivate them better than the Spirit of God!

God's abiding presence stays with your children forever. He will show them the best choice to make in every situation as they stay connected with Him. As they grow to love Him with all their heart, soul, mind and strength nothing will be able to motivate them better than the Spirit of God!

## Never Stop Trying!

If what you're consistently doing is not motivating your kids, *try another way*. Those are the three life-changing words every successful parent, spouse, and business person knows and acts on. If you need help, seek more counsel. If you need more creative ideas to motivate your kids, you can get involved in one of our parenting coaching programs or e-mail/fax us a question or join in on a teleconference call. Every problem in your life is caused by either a lack of wisdom or a lack of discipline to apply the wisdom you already know. Never stop trying!

**TAKE AWAY**

- WHAT ARE THE TOP 3 NUGGETS OF WISDOM YOU CAN TAKE AWAY FROM THIS CHAPTER?
- WHAT PRINCIPLES ARE YOU ALREADY DOING?
- WHICH ONES DO YOU NEED TO PRAY AND ASK GOD TO HELP YOU PUT INTO PRACTICE?

---

**PARENTING 101 RECAP**: The foundation for motivating your kids is a solid relationship between you and them—second only to a solid relationship with God. Other ways you can help them include teaching them to be thankful, establishing routines, and helping them stay focused. With these things in place and a readiness to reward them for obedience, you will be able to motivate them in the key areas of doing chores, eating healthy, and getting along with others.

# Chapter 6

# *How to Avoid Eight Common Parenting Pitfalls*

"The advice of a wise man refreshes like water from a mountain spring. Those accepting it become aware of the pitfalls on ahead."

— Proverbs 13:14 TLB

As parents, we all make mistakes. None of us *had* perfect parents, and none of us *will be* perfect parents. But we don't have to be perfect to succeed at raising great kids, we just have to keep learning and growing. Over the years, I have observed eight common problems that all parents run into at some time or another. In this chapter we will identify these parenting pitfalls and learn how to effectively overcome them.

**PITFALL #1**

## Yelling and Correcting Your Kids in Anger

The most common pitfall we face as parents is *yelling at our kids and correcting them in anger.* In life, there can be extraneous circumstances that cause us to be moody and irritable. Financial pressures, time constraints, physical exhaustion and the challenges of parenting can definitely cause our fuse to be shortened. Nevertheless, we can learn how to control our emotions and not take our frustrations out on our children. Scripture says, "He who is slow to anger is better than the mighty, he who rules his [own] spirit than he who takes a city" (Proverbs 16:32 AMP).

I have found that the main reasons we explode in anger and yell at our kids is because we have not been consistently applying predetermined consequences the first time our children act up. For example, we see that our daughter's room is a mess, so we tell her to clean it up and we continue on with whatever we are doing. A few hours later, her room is still a mess. We remind her again, "Let's get this room cleaned up." She says, "Okay. I will," but continues to play with her toys. More time passes, and the room remains untouched. We remind her a third time, and still nothing changes. At this point, we become enraged and explode, saying, "I've told you to clean this room all day! You never listen! I am so sick of this mess!"

> The most common pitfall we face as parents is yelling at our kids and correcting them in anger. "Human anger does not produce the righteousness God desires" (James 1:20 NLT).

The real issue here is not an obedience problem but a parenting problem. Disobedience must be addressed the first time it occurs, before we get upset. Assuming that you have already coached your children on how you expect their room to be cleaned, you can simply say, "Stop what you're doing now and go clean your room. Do not do anything else until it's done." With this controlled response, we can avoid exploding and the emotional damage to our children that comes with it. If they fail to obey, we must immediately enforce a consequence—one they should already know is coming.

Stop and think. What behaviors do your children do that really make you angry? You know, things they have done again and again in spite of your pleas to them to stop? Take time to sit down and come up with a specific consequence for each inappropriate behavior—a consequence that removes a privilege they enjoy. After you DIA (see Chapter 4) and write it down, tell your children, "The next time you do 'X,' 'Y' is going to happen."

Having set consequences for inappropriate behavior makes it easier to remain calm when your children misbehave. Instead of giving them a series of ineffective warnings, tell them *once* what you want them to do and remind them of the privilege they will enjoy when they are done. For example, say, "Clean your room so you can play for the rest of the afternoon." If they don't obey, take a deep breath and enforce the consequence. Consistency is the key.

Consequences that are enforced quickly and calmly deliver discipline that is remembered.

> Stop and think. What behaviors do your children do that really make you angry? Take time to sit down and come up with a specific consequence for each one. Having set consequences for inappropriate behavior makes it easier stay calm when they misbehave.

For me, controlling my anger and not yelling is one of the hardest things I have had to learn. My father was a yeller, so that is what was modeled for me. I have had to unlearn many methods I unconsciously developed. I continue to work with the Lord to be the patient father my kids need. I'm glad to say that with His help, I have gotten much better. I have learned to condition myself to make sure my voice stays calm when bringing my children correction. When I begin to get upset, my kids know it because my voice gets very quiet and my words are few. I usually tell everyone to go to their rooms so I can calm down and get God's wisdom on how I am to handle the situation.

Recently, I was having breakfast with my nineteen-year-old son just before he went back to college for his sophomore year. We were with another strong, mighty man of God who wanted to speak a blessing into my son's life before he left. In the course of the conversation, my friend asked him how I had changed over the years. My son replied, "Well, Dad stops and thinks before he says stuff now."

I sat back and thought about what he said. Then I replied, "That's because I'm silently praying to God for wisdom. I'm asking God to give me the words to say and to help me control my mouth and my temper so that I don't respond to my kids out of the impulse of my flesh." When I take time to think about what I'm going to say and go through the catalog of wisdom and experience God has given me, He shows me how to respond. It only takes a few seconds.

So don't blow up. It doesn't help anybody. Decide In Advance on the best consequences for your children's inappropriate behavior. You can also Decide In Advance to stop and ask God for help before you say something. God will grant you wisdom and grace to stay calm, cool and in control and follow through with what you said you would do.

Don't blow up. It doesn't help anybody. Decide In Advance (DIA) on the best consequences for your children's inappropriate behavior. Stop and ask God for help before you say anything. He will grant you wisdom and grace to stay calm, cool and in control.

## PITFALL #2

## Arguing and Quarreling

The second pitfall is *arguing and quarreling* with our kids. I'm always amazed when I see a parent arguing with their four- or five-year-old child. It's like a general arguing with a private or an NFL coach arguing with a water boy on the sideline. Think about it. People in authority don't argue with people underneath them. They simply tell them what to do. I don't ask my employees to do things or argue with them; I tell them what to do. When we argue, we relinquish our authority and enable our children's disobedience and rebellion.

Imagine that in your relationship with your children, you are on a very tall ladder. As the parent, you are positioned on rung 70, and your children are on rung 3. When you argue and quarrel with them, you have to walk 67 steps down the ladder to get to their level. In doing so, you have completely abdicated your position of authority. This is always a "lose-lose" situation because you can't win an argument with a child. It should never occur in the first place.

Let's say you tell your ten-year-old son, who has a pattern of procrastinating and making excuses, to stop playing video games, clean his room, and then go take a bath. He responds, "Okay, mom/dad." You return ten minutes later, and he is still playing video games. Greatly frustrated, you ask, "What are you doing, son? I told you to stop playing games, clean your room, and go take a bath."

"Yeah, but I was just about to win and move to the next level. I just wanted to finish this one game," he answers.

Annoyed, you respond, "What am I going to have to do to get you to listen to me?"

"I do listen to you," he says. "I just wanted to finish this game. Man, what's the big deal? Why are you getting so upset? Jimmy's parents don't treat him this way."

"What do Jimmy's parents have to do with you cleaning your room and going to take a bath?" you reply. "I don't think I'm too hard on you. I think I treat you very well."

"That's not true," he retorts. "You never let me have any fun. You're always riding my case about something."

"When do I ride your case?" you answer angrily. "What are you talking about? I'm just asking you to do what you need to do."

By this point the atmosphere is heated with emotion. You are trying to defend yourself to your son, and the argument is going nowhere fast. What he is really doing is trying to justify and deflect his disobedience. Arguing and trying to get your kids to see your side of things doesn't work.

> People in authority don't argue with people underneath them. They simply tell them what to do. If you argue with your kids, you relinquish your authority and come down to their level. This is always a "lose-lose" situation.

God says, "The servant of the Lord must not be quarrelsome (fighting and contending). Instead, he must be kindly to everyone and mild-tempered [*preserving the bond of peace*]; he must be a skilled and suitable teacher, patient and forbearing and willing to suffer wrong" (2 Timothy 2:24 AMP). Does this mean you let your kids walk all over you, saying whatever they want to say? No. It just means that as their teacher, you purpose in your heart and mind not to fight and argue with them about anything. You are the parent and they are the child. When you want them to do something, you calmly but firmly give them instruction. There is no room to negotiate. They have two choices: Obey *or* face the consequence of their disobedience.

If my kids start arguing with me, there is an automatic consequence. Why? Because arguing with one's parent is an attitude of disrespect and dishonor. It is the root cause of all rebellion and disobedience.

One of the rules at our house is that our young kids are allowed only one soda a week. Even in restaurants that offer endless refills, they still get only one soda. When they finish that, they get water. We have taught them the health issues that result from drinking too much soda. So, if they start to complain, I say, "That's the way we do things in our house. If one is not enough, you can have no soda at all. But we are not going to argue about it." The amazing thing is, now that we have trained our kids in this area, when the waitress comes back and offers them refills, they tell her on their own, "No thanks. I'd just like some water now." It's so rewarding to see the training you have instilled come out in their behavior.

The bottom line is, you don't need to argue with your kids, and you shouldn't. It is pointless and only serves to stir up strife. Once you have prayerfully made the house rules, they are not up for discussion. What you say goes. Take your position of authority and hold firmly to it. Decide In Advance what the consequences will be for arguing, and follow through with them if they cross the line. Doing this will give you more peace with your children and in your home.

> You are the parent and they are the child. When you want your kids to do something, you calmly but firmly give them instruction. There is no room to negotiate. They have two choices: Obey *or* face the consequence of their disobedience.

## PITFALL #3
# Over-explaining Things

Watch out for the dangerous pitfall of *over-explaining things*. This is a major issue for the mom or dad who thinks that if they can just get their children to understand the "why" behind the house rules, they would be willing to obey. The problem is you can't put a thirty-five-year-old head on the shoulders of a five- or six-year-old. You can attempt to explain things to your kids for hours on end, but they are not going to get it.

Many times parents over-explain themselves to their children because they are insecure. They are fearful of being rejected by them or being too hard on them. Sometimes they just feel inadequate. A parent may think: *What if they reject me? I don't want them to think I don't love them. I don't want them to think I'm mean or too strict or old-fashioned.* It really doesn't matter what your kids think about the way you discipline them. You don't have to answer to them for the way you discipline; you have to answer to God.[1] They won't understand the "why" behind everything you do, and they don't have to. They simply need to honor and obey.

The Bible says, "Children, obey your parents; this is the right thing to do because God has placed them in authority over you. Honor your father and mother. This is the first of God's Ten Commandments that ends with a promise. And this is the promise: that if you honor your father and mother, yours will be a long life, full of blessing" (Ephesians 6:1-3 TLB). Notice that God doesn't say, "Children, obey your parents and honor them *if you understand and agree with what they are telling you.*" He simply says, "Obey them and honor them."

> It doesn't matter what your kids think about the way you discipline them. You don't have to answer to them; you have to answer to God. They won't understand the "why" behind everything you do, and they don't have to. They simply need to honor and obey.

Over-explaining and arguing with your kids partners with their disobedience. They do not need to understand or agree with your rules to follow them. For example, I was in the store recently and I saw a woman and her daughter in the checkout line, surrounded by gum, candy bars, and a few small toys. Suddenly, little "Stacy's" eyes locked in on a candy bar. She grabbed it and held it high with a smile.

At this, the mother said, "Stacy, I told you before we got here that you couldn't have a candy bar. Put it back."

"No!" Stacy replied, crossing her arms.

Slightly irritated, the mother said, "Stacy, you've got to put the candy bar back. You can't have a candy bar today."

Again, Stacy refused, "No!"

At this point, the hopeful mother began to try to reason with her daughter, saying, "Stacy, every time we come to the store we go through this, and I'm tired of it. You can't have candy. Candy is not good for you. It's going to give you a tummy ache, and it's bad for your teeth. You're going to get cavities and have to go to the dentist."

"No!" Stacy defiantly uttered.

With obedience nowhere in sight, the mother resorted to threatening the little girl. "Stacy, if you don't put that candy bar back, I'm going to tell your father you didn't listen to me and he's going to give you a spanking when he gets home. And you won't be able to play with your friends either." But Stacy wouldn't budge, and the standoff escalated into a yelling match, embarrassing the mother and making Stacey cry.

> Over-explaining and arguing with your kids partners with their disobedience. They do not need to understand or agree with your rules to follow them.

Sound familiar? I see situations like this all the time, but it doesn't have to be that way. You can get your kids to listen the first time without over-explaining your rules by guiding them to the behavior you want. For example, let's say you find yourself in the same situation as Stacy's mom. Your daughter picks up a candy bar and you say, "I told you before we got here that you couldn't have any candy. Put it back." The moment she says, "No," or she doesn't move, reach over, take the candy bar from her hand, and put it back.

Let's say you tell your son, "Pick up your dirty clothes and brush your teeth. Bedtime is in five minutes," but he doesn't move. He stays on the floor coloring. Walk over to him, *calmly* close his coloring book and say, "Come on, son. Let's go and get started." What are you doing? You are guiding your child to the behavior you want. You are not over-explaining, yelling, or arguing. You tell them once, and then calmly, physically assist them in the desired direction after the first command.

They must learn to honor and obey you when you first give instruction. This pleases God and sets them up for a long, blessed life.

> Don't over-explain your instructions to your kids. They are not going to get it. Calmly, clearly, and assertively enforce first-time obedience by guiding them to the behavior you want. They must learn to honor and obey you when you first give instruction.

**PITFALL #4**

## Parenting Out of Fear

The fourth pitfall we must recognize and avoid falling into is *parenting our kids out of fear*. This is one trap that is not always easy to detect. Fear comes in many forms, including anxiety, worry, doubt, insecurity, and being overly concerned with what others think of us. When fear is motivating our parenting, it is often accompanied by these symptoms:

a lack of peace, feelings of pressure, and confusion. Fear in any form is not from God. "For God has not given us a spirit of fear, but of power and of love and of a sound mind" (2 Timothy 1:7 NKJV). With His help we can learn to identify and eliminate any parenting that is motivated by fear.

A good place to start looking to determine if you are parenting out of fear is your childhood. How were you parented? What type of things happened to you? Did you get spanked or screamed at excessively? Were you locked in closets as punishment? Were you ignored or given the silent treatment for days on end? These experiences carry not only pain but also fear, and if these hurts and fears are not dealt with, they will subtly influence the way you discipline your kids. Many times parents will withhold discipline from their children to keep them from experiencing the same pain they felt as kids. Because their parents were unable to discipline them without inflicting physical or emotional pain, they see discipline as a hurtful thing and avoid giving it to their own children.

Just because your mom and dad misused some forms of discipline and took them to extremes doesn't mean you should abandon them altogether. That's like vowing to never go to a doctor because you or someone you know had a bad experience with one. There is wisdom you can gather from the discipline you experienced. You don't have to parent your kids from the ghosts of your past, afraid that you will cause them emotional distress or crush their self-esteem or be rejected by them.

> Fear comes in many forms, including anxiety, worry, doubt, insecurity, and being overly concerned with what others think. When fear is motivating our parenting, it is often accompanied by a lack of peace, feelings of pressure, and confusion. Fear in any form is not from God.

Let me give you an example. When I was growing up, I was often humiliated by my dad in front of my friends. He would yell at me and insult me in front of them. It hurt and embarrassed me deeply. As a result, I never wanted to do the same thing to my kids. Fear of repeating what my dad did to me could have kept me from disciplining my kids when they were with their friends, even though they needed it. Instead, I have learned to call them into another room and speak with them privately. I calmly say, "Come here, please. I need to talk to you for a minute." Once we are away from their friends, I tell them what they need to do. For example, I may say, "You need to be more respectful of your mother. You and your friends need to quiet down and pick things up. If not, they will have to go home. Now go out there and make sure you are all behaving correctly." This eliminates the humiliation but provides the discipline they need. Praise your kids in public; correct them in private.

Another way we can parent out of fear is by being afraid of how our kids will react when we correct them. I've seen many parents worry that their kids will think they are too strict or mean. Others will withhold discipline because they are afraid their kids will refuse to give them affection or they will throw a major fit if they don't get their way. They think, *What if my son throws a fit in the middle of the restaurant if I tell him he can't have a dessert? What will I do? I will be so embarrassed.*

Correct him, and if he throws a fit, throw him over your shoulder and carry him out of the restaurant to your car. Once you are in the car say, "Because of your poor behavior, you will not be going to another restaurant until you are more mature. You have lost the privilege of eating out." Then get him a sitter the next few times the family goes out to eat. The pain of the consequence is what teaches children not to repeat the wrong behavior. The key is to administer the discipline in love, letting the consequence do the work, not harsh words or hurtful hands. "No discipline is enjoyable while it is happening—it's painful! But afterward there will be a peaceful harvest of right living for those who are trained in this way" (Hebrews 12:11 NLT).

One of the most effective consequences for inappropriate behavior is to remove a big, long-anticipated privilege, such as going to a friend's birthday party. Once you have exhausted other avenues of correction and your children's behavior still hasn't improved, you must give them a consequence that is going to get their attention. My own kids have pushed the limits of my tolerance to see if I would take away a big privilege they had been waiting for. It surprised them when I did and they never forgot the lesson. I just looked at them calmly and said, "I'm sorry but because of your poor behavior this past week and your refusal to respond to correction, you can't go to your friend's birthday party." This type of consequence is painful for your children and painful for you to enforce, but once you do it, you will probably never have to go to that extreme again.

> The pain of the consequence is what teaches children not to repeat the wrong behavior. The key is to administer the discipline in love, letting the consequence do the work, not harsh words or hurtful hands.

You may be thinking, *But Mike, why would you do that? Isn't that going to hurt the birthday kid? What will his parents think?* To be quite blunt, I couldn't care less. The birthday kid is going to have several other children at the party. Drop off his present and he'll be fine. Training my children is more important than the temporary disappointment of their friends or what the other child's parents think of me. I cannot allow the fear of not being accepted by others dictate how I raise my kids. Neither can you. We are responsible to God to train up our children in the way they should go. We will talk more about overcoming the fear of man in Chapter 7, but for now understand that we need to do what is right for those who are under our God-given authority.

Instead of being motivated by fear, God wants us to be motivated by *faith*. This means that when we bring correction to our kids, we *believe* in our heart that what we are saying and doing is right and in their best interest. It also means we believe we have God's blessings on our actions. Fear is the opposite of faith. When we parent our kids out of fear, we open the door for the enemy to work in their lives. When we parent our kids out of faith, we open the door for God to work in their lives. The source of our motivation affects the lives of everyone in our home and the very atmosphere in which we live. Either faith or fear will be released by our choice.

So don't be afraid to discipline your children for any reason. If you are afraid, they will sense it and use it to manipulate and control you. In each situation, pray and ask God for guidance and the confidence to do what you know in your heart is right.

> God wants you to be motivated by *faith* in your parenting. This means that when you bring correction to your kids, you *believe* in your heart that what you are saying and doing is right and in their best interest. It also means you believe you have God's blessings on your actions.

## PITFALL #5

# Making Threats and Not Following Through

Pitfall number 5 is *threatening our kids and not following through.* Like Stacy's mom in the earlier example, many parents resort to issuing empty threats when their children don't listen. *The Facts of Life* TV star Lisa Whelchel accurately describes the true value of threats. She says, "Threats will only teach kids the art of gambling. They ask themselves, *Will Mom really follow through this time?* Children know when the odds are in their favor, when it's worth the risk to push the limits." Think about it. Did your parents threaten you? How did it make you feel when they didn't follow through? How do you think it makes your kids feel? That's right—they lose respect for you.

By making empty threats to our kids and not following through, we are sending them a dangerous message. Indirectly we are saying, "There are no consequences for breaking the rules." By speaking threats and not following through, we are setting our kids up to be irresponsible in all areas of life. I know young people who have shown up late for work again and again or who regularly didn't meet their deadlines, and then were surprised when they got fired. What's even worse, by making threats and not following through we ultimately imply that God won't follow through on the consequences for sin He outlines in the Bible.

By speaking threats and not following through, we are setting our kids up to be irresponsible in all areas of life. What's even worse is that we ultimately imply that God won't follow through on the consequences for sin He outlines in the Bible.

Jesus made a powerful charge to us in Matthew 5:37. He said, "Let your Yes be simply Yes, and your No be simply No; anything more than that comes from the evil one" (AMP). In other words, we need to *say what we mean* and *mean what we say*. If we tell our children that they are going to receive a specific consequence for acting inappropriately, then we should follow through with it. This goes back to the importance of Deciding In Advance what the consequences are going to be and calmly enforcing them. If we fail to plan, we can plan to fail.

Open-ended consequences can also assist us in keeping our word with the simple phrase "until further notice." When my teenagers' attitude or behavior took a major nosedive, I would say, "Okay, guys. No more electronics *until further notice.* No TV or video games, no iPods or iPhones, no cell phones, and no music. You'll get your electronic privileges back when your attitude/behavior improves." I like to call this consequence "Going Amish," and boy, does it get their attention. "Until further notice" gives you flexibility and does not tie you to an unjust length of consequences spoken in the heat of the moment.

So say what you mean and mean what you say. Don't make empty threats and fail to follow through. This will help you gain and maintain credibility with your kids and add stability to your relationships. Once you start regularly enforcing the consequences you set, yelling and arguing will decrease and you won't feel the need to over-explain things. That's the synergistic effect of good parenting.

> Don't make empty threats and fail to follow through. Say what you mean and mean what you say. This will help you gain and maintain credibility with your kids and add stability to your relationships.

## PITFALL #6

# Trying to Be Their Best Friend

*Trying to be our children's best friend* is the next parenting pitfall we should be mindful of. Friends they have, its parents that they need. God has given you and me this critical role in our children's lives, and we must not surrender it.

I love my kids, and I am their friend. But I'm not their best friend. Best friends are on the same level. They share the confidential issues of their hearts with each other and give advice, but one is not in a position of authority over the other.

If you and I choose to be best friends with our children, we come down to their level just like when we argue with them. As a result, it is impossible to fully function as their parent, teaching them and enforcing consequences. Yes, we are to love them, hug them, kiss them, praise them, care for them, and bond with them in an appropriate way. But we are not to come down to their level for any reason. If we do, we abdicate our position of authority and protection and leave them vulnerable to the enemy.

For years, I have told my sons, "I'm your dad. We can be best friends when you are married and you have a mortgage." I have said this so many times that they now recite it back to me. A few times they have started joking around with me inappropriately. Immediately I stopped them and said, "Hey guys, save that for your buddies in the locker room. You are not going to joke around with me that way or mock me. Remember, I'm your father." To allow your kids to treat you as their best friend subtly opens the door to disrespect—a door you definitely need to keep shut.

Are there areas in your kids' lives where you would rather be their best friend than their parent? If you are telling off-color jokes, watching inappropriate movies and TV shows with them, hanging out with them and their friends, or sharing your personal issues with them you are setting the stage for major problems. As their best friend, you forfeit the honor, respect, and authority you need to bring correction and direction to their lives. Yes, be a friend they can confide in; let them know they can come and talk to you about anything that is going on in their lives. But you must maintain a clear boundary, showing that you are their parent *first* and their friend second.

You and your kids are not on equal footing. You are the general, and they are the privates and lieutenants. Build your relationship by pressing in with love, words of praise, appropriate physical affection, and spending quality time together. But make sure the parent-child boundary stays in place.

> By trying to be your children's best friend, you forfeit the honor, respect, and authority you need to bring correction and direction to their lives. You must maintain a clear boundary, showing that you are their parent *first* and their friend second.

## PITFALL #7
## Asking Instead of Telling

*Asking our kids to do things instead of telling them* is pitfall #7. This unhealthy tendency is often closely linked with pitfalls four and six. If we are trying to be our children's best friend, we are going to have an inclination to ask them to do things instead of telling them. In most cases, *fear* is the motivation behind this form of parenting. It could be a fear of confrontation. Some parents I know are intimidated by their kids because of their strong personalities or size. Others are afraid of being rejected by their kids and/or want to be liked by them. This is insecurity and can be especially difficult when parents are divorced and feel the need to compete for their children's affections.

Parents who have fallen into this pitfall of *asking* instead of telling make statements like: "Would you please clean your room?" "Would you please do your homework?" "When you get a chance, could you please take out the trash?" Give me a break! This communication is fine between two coworkers or friends who are on the same level, but it's not the way parents direct their children. Instructions to our kids should sound more like, "Hey guys, go clean your room. Thanks," and "Get that homework done first, and then you can go out and play," and "Son, it's your day to take out the garbage. Please knock that out before you go to school, buddy."

Don't get me wrong. I am not saying we should walk around the house and bark orders at our kids like a drill sergeant. We should model good manners and say *please* and *thank you* and "speak the truth in love" as the Bible says.[2] But, as parents, we should not ***ask*** our children to carry out their chores. *Asking* gives them the option of saying no, and no is not an option. We need to communicate our instructions in a straightforward way. You will be amazed how your children will respond differently when you use different language. It's not necessarily what you say but how you say it. If you have been asking your kids to do things instead of telling them, change what you are saying.

As parents, we should not ask our children to carry out their chores. Asking gives them the option of saying no, and no is not an option. We need to communicate our instructions in a straightforward way.

One of the secrets to successful communication when giving commands is creating an *illusion of choice*. Children love to feel as if they have a choice in what they have to do. For example, let's say you want your child to take a bath. You can say, "Would you like to take your bath now or in five minutes?" This creates an illusion of choice. They are going to take their bath. You are just giving them a five-minute option, which works to diffuse their fight. Let's say you want them to get dressed for bed. You can tell them, "Put on your night clothes. Would you prefer the Spider-man pajamas or the Batman pajamas?" It's an illusion of choice, because either way, they are going to get dressed for bed.

The bottom line: Don't ask your kids to do things. *Tell them.* Asking waters down your discipline and diminishes the strength of your authority. Eliminate the weak, namby-pamby requests and give them the solid, straightforward directions they need.

**PITFALL #8**

## Over-commitment to Activities and Sports

The last parenting pitfall I want to talk about is allowing our kids to be *over-committed to hobbies and sports.* Kids today are involved in too many extracurricular activities. They are in Scouts, tennis lessons, karate, gymnastics, music lessons, football, baseball and soccer. Some children are doing something every night of the week, and their parents wear it like a badge of honor. But being that busy is not good for any family. If kids are gone for two or three hours every night, they are going to be under pressure to get their homework done. They are going to eat too much fast food and miss out on family mealtimes together. Over-commitment saps the energy and joy out of life and leaves mothers, fathers and children worn-out and relationally disconnected from each other.

There are a number of reasons why parents over schedule their kids, ranging from wanting their kids to try everything they are interested in to fear of not developing their child's gifts and talents to personal pride. Whatever the reason, it is not worth it. Being over-committed in multiple activities and sports for short periods of time tends to keep kids confined to the beginner's stage, never allowing them to rise above average in anything. We might say they become a jack-of-all-trades and master of none. And mastering a skill is very important—it's the fertile soil in which confidence and self-esteem grow.

Over-commitment saps the energy and joy out of life. It leaves mothers, fathers and children worn-out and relationally disconnected from each other. It is also a major cause for a lack of focus.

What I recommend is allowing your children to try as many different activities and sports as they want on a rotating schedule until they are about eight or ten. Let them experience baseball, basketball, dancing, gymnastics, swimming, music, art, you name it. As they do, take note of the activities they enjoy and excel at—the things they are talented in and passionate about. This is a major indicator of the way they are "bent" or shaped. You and your spouse, or just you if you are a single parent, should prayerfully decide which activities you believe provide the greatest benefits to your children and encourage them to go in that direction.

Our son Austin chose football and baseball and played them during different seasons of the school year. In the summer months he did art. Once Austin reached high school, he fully shifted his attention to football and karate. Our other son, Jake, initially chose fall wrestling and guitar all year and summers in art. His junior year in high school, he began an intense course of study in the AP gifted program, and his main focus became academics and karate. Our older daughter, Jessica, chose volleyball and academics. Shea, our youngest child, is now eight. She is devoted to ballet, but is also exploring her interest in horseback riding, music and art.

Some activities are better than others. They provide more value. I believe a quality martial arts program is one of the best things for a child. My children have been consistently practicing martial arts since they were four years old. Don't get me wrong. Sports like baseball, soccer and gymnastics provide great opportunities for physical fitness, coordination, and learning how to work as a team. But the instructors don't ask the child about how he is treating his parents or how he is doing in school. They don't teach kids to respect their mom and dad, be a person of integrity and do their chores cheerfully. Quality martial arts programs provide leadership training and development of life skills not as a side benefit, but as a primary emphasis. I highly recommend finding a well-balanced, professional martial arts school for your kids.

I recommend allowing your kids to try out for as many different activities and sports as they want until they are about eight or ten years old. As they do, take note of the things they enjoy and excel at. This is a major indicator of the way they are "bent" or shaped. Encourage them to go in that direction.

So how many clubs, sports and activities should your children participate in? Once they reach the age of ten, I suggest that they be doing no more than two extra-curricular activities at a time. Why is it important to make your kids focus on two or three things? I will answer that question with this "tale of two boys."

Meet "Stephen" and his friend "John." Both started karate at the same time. After about six months in the basic course, John's parents decided to drop karate and move him to tennis. Stephen signed up for another six months of karate. At the end of those six months, John dropped out of tennis and joined the local soccer team. Stephen signed up for a second year of karate. Another year passed, and John decided he wanted to start playing the guitar. Stephen signed up for another year of karate and earned his brown belt that year. At the end of three years, Stephen was well on his way to achieving his black belt in karate—the expert stage of competency. He went through plateaus and valleys and learned to focus and persevere. John, on the other hand, did not get out of the beginner stage in anything. He received limited experience in karate, tennis, soccer, and guitar and now lacks both focus and perseverance.

Picture it like this. You have a glass pitcher full of competitive juice and focus. If you pour it out into ten juice glasses, a very small amount goes into each one. If you pour it into five juice glasses, the strength of the competitive juice and focus is greater, but not as potent as it can be. If you pour it into two full-size glasses, you are going to get the greatest concentration of focus and success. My point is: you cannot spread out your kids' focus too thinly and expect success. By dividing their focus, you have diminished their ability to succeed. Jumping from one activity to another leads to lack of confidence and lack of accomplishment.

You cannot spread out your kids' focus too thinly and expect success. By dividing their focus, you have diminished their ability to succeed. Jumping from one activity to another leads to lack of confidence and lack of accomplishment.

So when your kids are little, let them try a variety of activities and sports to discover what they are good at and what they enjoy. Once they are about ten, narrow their participation to two activities at a time and let them master them. Don't let coaches, neighbors, friends, or grandparents push your kids into too many activities. If your children want to try something different, tell them, "I'm sorry, honey. We just don't have enough time in our schedule right now to add another activity. Maybe we can try that in the summer." Keep them focused. Help them to push through the plateau and valley stages of boredom and difficulty that come with any long-term endeavor. Don't let them quit when things get tough. Keep them balanced and control their schedule!

If you have fallen into one or more of these parenting pitfalls, get up and keep going. You are not a failure. The Bible says "...for though a righteous man falls seven times, he rises again..."(Proverbs 24:16 NIV). Keep learning, praying, and growing. You will make better decisions and see better results.

**TAKE AWAY**

- WHAT ARE THE TOP 3 NUGGETS OF WISDOM YOU CAN TAKE AWAY FROM THIS CHAPTER?
- WHAT PRINCIPLES ARE YOU ALREADY DOING?
- WHICH ONES DO YOU NEED TO PRAY AND ASK GOD TO HELP YOU PUT INTO PRACTICE?

---

**PARENTING 101 RECAP:** The eight common pitfalls of parenting we want to remember are: (1) Don't yell at your kids or correct them in anger. Stay calm, cool and in control. (2) Avoid arguing and quarreling. You are the General. (3) Don't over-explain things. Over-explaining partners with their disobedience. (4) Watch out for correcting your kids out of fear in any form. (5) Avoid making threats and not following through. Be consistent with consequences. (6) Don't try to be your children's best friend. Friends they have; it is parents they need. (7) Don't ask your kids to do things. Take the leadership role and tell them what to do. (8) Avoid over-commitment. Choose two or three sports or activities and let your kids master them.

# Chapter 7

# *Developing Seven Characteristics of an All-Star Parent*

"May you always be filled with the fruit of your salvation—the righteous character produced in your life by Jesus Christ —for this will bring much glory and praise to God."

— Philippians 1:11 NLT

What comes to mind when you hear the word *all-star*? Maybe words like *excellent, outstanding*, and *cream of the crop*. In sports, all-stars are the top players in their game. These are the standout athletes who have worked hard, studied their game, applied themselves fully to their position and reaped the rewards.

Similarly, there is a higher level of leaders in the home—the class I call *all-star parents*. These are real moms and dads like you and me who work diligently, study their "game," and apply themselves fully to their positions. What qualities set these all-star parents apart from the rest? There are seven specific characteristics that make an all star parent—qualities and skills you can develop in yourself.

**#1**

## Establish a Good Spiritual Foundation

The first and most important quality of all-star parents is that they purposely *establish a good spiritual foundation*—in their lives and the lives of their children. Repeatedly, we have touched on the importance of prayer and turning to God for help. It is only through Him that we have the ability to employ the power of praise, harness the power of our words, and create effective consequences and then follow through with them. He is the source of all wisdom, strength, direction, self-control, peace, and love who enables us to raise happy, obedient children.

> The first and most important quality of all-star parents is that they purposely *establish a good spiritual foundation*—in their lives and the lives of their children. God is the source of all wisdom, strength, direction, self-control, peace, and love who enables us to raise happy, obedient kids.

When we stay connected with God, we have access to everything we need to grow and mature into all-star parents. The key is *staying connected*. This happens through personal Bible reading and study, prayer, godly friendships, and attending and serving in a vibrant Bible-based church. Once we have established a good spiritual foundation in our lives, we can help our children establish one in theirs. God instructs parents in Deuteronomy 6:6-9 to teach children His Word. He says, "These commandments that I give you today are to be upon your hearts. Impress them on your children. Talk about them when you sit at home and when you walk along the road, when you lie down and when you get up. Tie them as symbols on your hands and bind them on your foreheads. Write them on the doorframes of your houses and on your gates" (NIV).

Sharing your faith with your children is ***the*** most important thing you can do as a parent. How do you do it? Start by introducing them to God's love and the message of the Gospel when they are little. Read Bible stories and sing songs to them about the Lord. Take them to church regularly where they can learn about Jesus with children their age. Talk about God with your children, pointing out how His character is reflected in His creation.[1] As they grow, memorize scriptures together, especially on topics that they are dealing with in their lives. There is nothing greater to plant in their hearts than the Word of God. Look for special opportunities to connect them with God, like Sunday school classes, Christian summer camps, vacation Bible schools, Christian music concerts, and youth gatherings.

Keep in mind, your kids are always watching you. You are never *not* teaching them. The example you live speaks louder than words. The best way to show your kids that volunteering and serving others is important is by volunteering and serving others. You can show them that it's more blessed to give than to receive by helping orphans and widows and giving to the poor.[2]

What else can you do? Make sure they have relevant resources to draw from that nourish them at their age. The most important is a Bible translation they can understand. There are many great Bibles for children, youth, and teens that present the Word of God in today's language. Other resources include Christian music, books, and DVDs.

Pray together without ceasing. You can pray around the dinner table, as you put them to sleep, and during special family times. Pray for our country, our troops, for each member of the family, and for friends. As you go through your day, pray with them for people you pass as you drive, pray when you hear about someone with a need, and praise and thank God out loud for all the little things He does for your family each day.

If you are connected in an ongoing, personal relationship with God, building a spiritual foundation in your kids' lives will come naturally. Pray and ask

Him to bless your family with a fresh desire to know and serve Him. Ask Him to show you how to weave His Word into your daily conversations and apply it to everyday situations. As you build a strong spiritual foundation in your kids' lives they will be equipped with what they need to make it in today's world.

> Make sure your kids have relevant resources to draw from that nourish them at their age. The most important is a Bible translation they can understand. There are many great Bibles for children, youth, and teens that present the Word of God in today's language.

**#2**

## Study Parenting and Continue to Improve

The second characteristic of all-star parents is that they *study parenting and continue to improve* themselves. There is always room for improvement, and godly knowledge is the key. God said, "My people are destroyed for *lack of knowledge...*" (Hosea 4:6 NKJV). Without wisdom you can't succeed at anything, including parenting. Becoming a better mom or dad should always be a priority.

I always start off my parenting conferences with a series of questions like, "How many of you have a hobby? Who likes to hunt and fish? How about sports? Any ladies into crafts or home decorating?" At this point, people are smiling and hands are going up all around the room. I then ask, "How many of you have magazines, books, or DVDs about your hobbies?" Again, many hands are raised. Then I ask, "How many of you have magazines, books, DVDs, or CDs on being a good parent?" Sadly, very few hands, if any, go up. The point of this exercise is that being a parent is the most important job we have on this earth, yet we do little to prepare for it. Most of us bought a book on pregnancy and babies when we were expecting a child, but stopped there. Many parents wait until they have a major problem and then they go and get a book. But we should be continually learning through every stage of our children's development.

Second Timothy 2:15 (KJV) says, "Study to shew [show] thyself approved unto God, a workman that needeth not to be ashamed, rightly dividing the word of truth." The ultimate book on parenting is God's Word. There are countless examples throughout scripture that show us what to do and what not to do as parents. There are great insights we can learn from people like Abraham, the father of faith, and Jacob, the father of the twelve tribes of Israel, and God, the Father of us all. The Bible is a resource we should be reading on a regular basis.

> To be a great parent, you must study parenting and continue to improve. You should be continually learning through every stage of your children's development. The Bible is the ultimate book on parenting—a resource we should be reading on a regular basis.

What else can you do? Talk to people who have great kids and seek their counsel. A wise man listens to advice.[3] Proverbs 11:14 (NKJV) says, "Where there is no counsel, the people fall; but in the multitude of counselors there is safety." Talk with people who have kids in their twenties or thirties who are godly, successful in their careers, and have healthy marriages. Ask them how they raised their kids and you'll get some great wisdom. You can also seek wise counsel by going to parenting conferences, workshops, and small group studies. One nugget of wisdom can change the course of your parenting and the destiny of your children in ways you never dreamed.

I have heard people say, "Well, I'm the parent. I decide how it goes. I don't need help from anybody." This close-minded view reveals an attitude of pride, and "by pride comes nothing but strife, but with the well-advised is wisdom" (Proverbs 13:10 NKJV). I am still learning and growing as a father. I ask questions of those I respect, especially now that my two sons are in college. My relationship with them is very different today than when they were living at home. I'm more of a mentor and a coach, and I need new insights on how to stay connected and relate to them. By swallowing my pride and humbling myself before others who have walked where I haven't walked, God has shown me things and given me answers that have helped me improve in all areas of life.

> Talk to people who have great kids and seek their counsel. A wise man listens to advice. One nugget of wisdom can change the course of your parenting and the destiny of your children in ways you never dreamed.

To improve as a parent, you actually have to improve as a person. If you are married, this includes studying to improve as a husband or wife. Your parenting will only be as strong as your marriage. Let me illustrate with this example. With your arms down at your sides, bring your hands together and interlock your fingers, forming a cradle. This represents the relationship between husband and wife. The children born to this relationship sit within the cradle they form. Now slowly pull your hands apart. This represents the husband and wife drifting away from each other. Parents may not be physically separated or divorced, but their hearts and minds can become isolated from each other. What happens as your hands move apart? Cracks begin to form. As they do, the children cradled by the parents begin to fall through. Again, your parenting will only be as strong as your marriage.

So as you study to be a great parent, also study to be a great spouse. Read your Bible, seek wise counsel, and stay on top of your game. You will continually improve your parenting skills and the day will come when people will seek *your* wise counsel!

> To improve as a parent, you actually have to improve as a person. If you are married, this includes studying to improve as a husband or wife. Your parenting will only be as strong as your marriage.

## #3

# Become Immune to the Criticism of Others

*Becoming immune to the criticism of others* is another crucial quality we must learn to develop. As you begin to implement the principles you are learning, people are going to have an opinion about it—particularly your kids and relatives. The new guidelines, practices, and boundaries are definitely going to ruffle some feathers, so you must be ready for it. Some will applaud your choices, and others will criticize. If you expect some criticism, it won't bother you as much when you get it. But there is only one opinion that you should be concerned about, and that is God's.

As I have said before, God is the only one you will have to stand before and give an account to for your parenting.[4] If you are moved by what others think of you, you have fallen into the trap of *people pleasing*. The Bible calls this the fear of man, and it has a deadly choke hold on many parents in our culture today. Proverbs 29:25 (NLT) says, "Fearing people is a dangerous trap, but trusting the Lord means safety." This same verse in The Message reads,

"The fear of *human opinion* disables; trusting in God protects you from that." The fear of man is not a place of strength from which to parent. It is a position of weakness. Trusting God and pleasing Him in the way you discipline your kids is all that matters.

Now you may be thinking, *Mike, I thought you said it's important for us as parents to seek wise counsel from people who have great kids and are more mature in the Lord.* Yes, we are to seek wise counsel, but at the same time we cannot become overly concerned with what others think about us. Parenting is not a popularity contest. We cannot be swayed by the opinions of our parents, friends, or the parents of our children's friends. Typically, many of the people I talk to are worried that they will be perceived by others as too strict, hard-nosed or mean. But the bottom line is we can't let people's opinions dictate how we parent. We need to do what we feel in our heart is best for our kids and blessed by God.

Unfortunately, the majority of parents in our churches today have mediocre standards for their children. Some of them don't know any better, and some have simply grown weary of fighting the pull of our culture. Consequently, my kids sometimes say,

"Dad, that's not fair. The other kids get to do 'this/that'—even kids at church. And their parents are leaders." I tell them, "I don't care what other people are doing. I listen to God about how I am to raise you."

"Well, 'Steven's' going to the party," they respond.

To this I reply, "I'm not Steven's father. I'm your father, and this is how we're going to do it in the Storms' family." I never say we are better than another family nor do I let my kids say it. I say we are *different*.

> Parenting is not a popularity contest. You can't be swayed by the opinions of your parents, friends, or the parents of our children's friends. Trusting God and pleasing Him in the way you discipline your kids is all that matters.

Think about it. Have you ever given a consequence to your children but then changed it because you were getting negative feedback from family members or the parents of your children's friends? This is parenting pitfall number four, parenting your kids out of fear, which we talked about in the last chapter. Don't give in to that and don't try to defend your decision. Stand your ground in spite of what others think of you. Don't worry about pleasing your friends, your kids, or anybody else. Just please God. I know it's bold and it's drastic. But bold, drastic decisions produce bold, drastic change.

As an all-star parent, you have to become immune to the criticism of others. This is done by learning to consistently submit yourself to God and get His direction in every situation you face.[5] This is what it means to *fear the Lord*, and the "fear of the Lord is the foundation of true wisdom. All who obey his commandments will grow in wisdom." (Psalm 111:10 NLT). Only the fear of God can deliver you from the fear of man.

## #4

## Give Up Being Liked in Exchange for Being Respected

The fourth characteristic of all-star parents is they *give up being liked by their kids in exchange for being respected*. This quality is closely linked with becoming immune to the criticism of others and the pitfall of trying to be your kid's best friend. To respect someone is to hold them in high esteem and honor. When we respect someone, we place worth and value on them, admiring and appreciating who they are and what they have done. Respect is not something we automatically get from our kids. It must be earned over time.

If your children *like* you from the time they are born until they turn eighteen, you didn't stand for much and you didn't instill a lot of discipline in their lives. The fact is, when you establish rules and routines and consistently enforce consequences, they are not always going to like you. Children do not rejoice when they do not get what they want. They do not like the person who stands in the way of immediately gratifying their desires. But don't change your decision to try and make them happy. Their joy will only be temporary. Your adult child will not say things like, "Thanks, Mom, for letting me quit piano when I was eight because I was tired of practicing. You're the best!" or "Thanks, Dad, for letting me quit karate when I was six months away from black belt because I was scared to take the test. You rock!" or "Thanks for turning a blind eye to my drinking when I was a teenager so I could have all that fun." Instead, what they say is, "What were you thinking, Mom? Why did you let me quit? Why did you let me behave that way, Dad?" Parenting your kids so they like you always leads to a lack of respect and deep regret later on.

The biggest thing you can do to get your kids to respect you is to be consistent. Consistency creates credibility and trust in your relationship, out of which grows respect. Your children know the boundaries that are in place, which makes them feel confident, safe and secure. Once you establish trust and credibility, obedience takes root.

> Respect is not something we automatically get from our kids. It must be earned over time. The fact is, when you establish rules and routines and consistently enforce consequences, they are not always going to like you. But in the long run, they will respect you.

*Earning your children's respect* happens in an interesting way. It's like making an investment in something for years with no sign of any profit. Then suddenly it begins to pay great dividends. *Getting your kids to like you* is just the opposite. It pays up front but shows great loss in the end. If you do everything your kids want you to do and let them have everything they want to have, you would think they would love and respect you. However, the opposite is true. Oh, they will *like* you while you are giving them everything they want, but their feelings will be shallow, short lived, and absent of respect.

Imagine a kid living in Beverly Hills. His parents give him a BMW and he wrecks it. Then they buy him a Mercedes, and eventually he wrecks it as well. No consequences are given out for his inappropriate behavior, and he is allowed to go out and party all weekend long during his high school years. His parents don't really care where he is, who he is with or what hour he gets home. By the time he reaches the age of twenty, he will have no respect for them and little or no relationship with them. On the other hand, the kid whose parents established and enforced rules, made him work to buy his own car, and required him to be home by eleven or midnight on weekends will have great respect for his parents and a good relationship with them when he reaches age twenty. Through consistent discipline, love has been shown and a bond of respect has been forged—a bond that will last a lifetime.

Unconsciously, children see and associate consistently enforced boundaries with love. Your willingness to do what is right for your kids, not what is easy, will earn their respect over time. Choose to invest consistent, loving discipline in their lives up front, and it will pay off big time in the years ahead.

Your willingness to do what is right for your kids, not what is easy, will earn their respect over time. Choose to invest consistent, loving discipline in their lives up front, and it will pay off big time in the years ahead.

**#5**

## Recognize Bad Behavior and Expect Obedience

The fifth characteristic of all-star parents is that they *recognize bad behavior and expect obedience.* This is so important. How can we recognize bad attitudes and behavior? We can't use the criterion of right and wrong modeled by the media or the American culture. It is constantly changing for the worse. We need a set standard. The only absolute standard of right and wrong is the Word of God. It is the ultimate measuring stick by which we are to evaluate our children's behavior.

Psalm 119:89 says, "What you say goes, God, and stays, as permanent as the heavens. Your truth never goes out of fashion; it's as up-to-date as the earth when the sun comes up. Your Word and truth are dependable as ever" (The Message). This same truth is echoed by Jesus in Matthew 24:35 and Peter in 1 Peter 1:25. Not only is God's Word everlasting, it is also all-powerful. It is the instruction manual that transforms the lives of our children. "The whole Bible was given to us by inspiration from God and is useful to teach us what is true and to make us realize what is wrong in our lives; it straightens us out and helps us do what is right. It is God's way of making us well prepared at every point, fully equipped to do good to everyone" (2 Timothy 3:16,17 TLB). The more we are in the Word, the quicker we are going to recognize bad behavior in our children and be able to bring the necessary correction that produces obedience.

When you talk to your kids about right and wrong behavior, let the Bible back you up. For example, if your son is having a problem with lying, tell him, "God loves you, Son. He hates lying, but He loves when you tell the truth."[7] By using Scripture to back up what you are saying, you direct your children's focus toward God. You help them see that the rule you have established and are enforcing is not just mom and dad's opinion. It is God's unchanging Word.

> The only absolute standard of right and wrong is the Word of God. The more we are in the Word, the quicker we are going to recognize bad behavior in our children and be able to bring the necessary correction that produces obedience.

Not only do we have God's Word to help us recognize bad behavior, we also have the gift of His Spirit. One of the Spirit's primary jobs is to lead and guide us into all truth,[6] which includes the truth about what is going on in our children's lives. The most common way He leads us is by *peace*. Colossians 3:15 (AMP) says, "And let the **peace** (soul harmony which comes) from Christ rule (*act as umpire continually*) in your hearts [deciding and settling with finality all questions that arise in your minds...]." If you don't have peace about something your son or daughter has said or done, it is probably a red flag to get your attention. Go to them and say, "Hey, we need to talk about that thing you said/did last night. That was out of line." The purpose of God withdrawing His peace from you is so you will address the wrong behavior. Listen for His still, small voice.

The best time to correct inappropriate behavior in your kids is when it starts. Every wrong attitude and action starts small. You've seen it—they give a smart little comment here, a little disrespect there. They utter a long sigh, roll their eyes, stomp their feet, or slam a door. These are the kinds of things you have to recognize right away and nip in the bud. Don't ignore their little rumblings and grumblings. Cut them off as soon as you see them so they don't have a chance to grow into something worse.

While we are to recognize bad behavior in all its forms, we are still to look for the best in our kids and not the worst. This is part of what it means to be a good finder—to *expect obedience.* God doesn't want us to expect our children to do wrong, He wants us to expect them to do right. With this mind-set, we are ready, willing, and waiting to reward good behavior.

> If you don't have peace about something your son or daughter has said or done, it is probably the Holy Spirit trying to get your attention. Listen to His still, small voice.

#6

# Become an Expert at Creating Fun-Filled Family Moments

Another quality all-star parents have is the ability to *create fun-filled family moments.* These are the lighthearted times of togetherness that everyone enjoys. Smiles illuminate faces, laughter fills the air, and family members reconnect. Nothing lightens the load of life like laughter. It's contagious and changes the atmosphere of the home like few things can. Proverbs 17:22 (NLT) says, "A cheerful heart is good medicine, but a broken spirit saps a person's strength." Becoming an expert at creating fun-filled family moments is a powerful gift to develop.

Now, when I counsel people on this subject, the first objection I usually hear is, "Well, we don't have the money to go on fancy vacations and do those kinds of things." But that's not what I'm talking about. Having fun is not about spending a lot of money. It's about generating laughter, love, and genuine joy within the family. You can have a teddy bear tea party or build a indoor tent with blankets. You can play tag in the front yard or run in the rain and make great memories. You can pull out board games and enjoy a family game night or pop some popcorn and watch a couple of your favorite movies. Creating fun-filled moments can be anything from throwing a Frisbee or a football, to making a craft together or playing a game of hopscotch. The list of things you can do is endless, and they don't have to cost a lot of money. Get creative!

> Having fun is not about spending a lot of money. It's about generating laughter, love and genuine joy within the family. The list of things you can do together as a family is endless, and they don't have to cost a lot.

Parents need to find out about what activities are important to their kids and begin doing them. Is it playing hide-and-seek or board games, walking the dog, or riding bikes? Is it reading together, doing a puzzle, or looking through old family photos? All these things are free. What about your local community? What fun things can you do together as a family? How about going to a museum, having a picnic in the park, hiking a nearby nature trail, or going for a swim? In most cases, these things cost nothing but provide priceless opportunities to connect.

How about family vacations? They don't have to be expensive to be fun. You can drive an hour or two, rent a cabin for a couple of nights, and have a blast. If the beach is close by, you can plan a two- or three-night getaway for your family to enjoy. You might be thinking, *Mike, I don't know where to go. I don't think there's anything close by for us to do.* Well, get a map of your state or region and sit around the table with your kids and spouse and explore it together. Half the fun of going on a trip is planning it. Looking at maps and brochures of places to visit are moments you and your kids will remember forever. You're making memories!

Fun-filled family moments are the glue that bonds you together. So find out what kind of things your children and spouse enjoy and get them on your calendar. Talk with other parents and get ideas of what they do for fun. Contact your local chamber of commerce or tourism office and find out the things you can do nearby that are free or have a minimal cost. Make sure your house is a fun place to be that is full of laughter. Realize that when your kids are happy and there is a balance of fun and great relationships coupled with discipline, they are easier to coach. It's about having fun, laughing, and being connected.

> Fun-filled family moments are the glue that bonds you together. Realize that when your kids are happy and there is a balance of fun and great relationships coupled with discipline, they are easier to coach. Its about having fun, laughing and being connected.

**#7**

## Teach Your Kids to Appreciate and Value Their Family

The last characteristic of all-star parent is that they *teach their kids to appreciate and value their family*. This means passing on your family heritage and history and sharing details about your ancestry, family traditions, and the hardships your people overcame. Are there any famous people in your family tree? What country did your great, great grandparents come from? How did your past generations celebrate the holidays? Which relatives were closest to God? This information is vital to helping children understand who they are and where they came from. Valuing family also includes communicating the importance of looking out for one another and protecting the family name. All of these things work together to teach children honor, respect, and gratitude. They help break down generational walls and open up communication between family members.

My wife and I share stories about the people in our family with our kids whenever the opportunity arises. We have relatives who have served our country in the military all the way back to the Revolutionary War. In every generation, someone in our family line has fought to protect the freedoms we cherish. My father was a marine, and I was a marine too. Do you have relatives who served in the military or as firefighters or policemen? Are there educators, inventors, pastors, nurses, or business entrepreneurs in your family? This is your heritage and history. These are the people your children need to know about. They are the real-life heroes they can truly be proud of. Share their stories with your kids. If they are still alive, set up times to get together with them so your children can hear their stories firsthand. Your children's hearts will be inspired, and the real-life heroes in your family will feel valued and loved.

> Teaching your kids to appreciate and value their family means passing on your family heritage and history. It also includes communicating the importance of looking out for one another and protecting the family name.

As a family, it is also important that everyone looks out for and takes care of one another. We teach our kids that God comes first, then family, then school. When our children were little, we told them, "Nobody is more important than family. You have to stand by your brother and sister. Make sure no one picks on them. And never pick on each other." Fighting within the family is something we don't tolerate and neither should you. A house that is divided against itself cannot stand.[8] Preserving unity is priority.[9] We need more moms and dads teaching this to their children.

Protecting your family name is also vital. No one should talk about family business at school, at church, or anywhere else—not even with other friends. Things that are confidential and personal should not be blabbed all over town. For example, if one of your children has a problem with wetting the bed, this is family business that is confidential. If mom or dad got a speeding ticket, it is personal information that should be kept within the family. Clearly communicate to your kids what kinds of things you consider confidential and make sure they understand. This is not about keeping secrets. It is about respecting private information.

Family appreciation and knowing one's heritage and history is not something that just happens. It is something that has to be taught. So think about the things you treasure most about your family heritage and begin to pass them on to your children. This kind of communication produces great appreciation and connectivity within the family.

> Teach your kids that God comes first, then family, then school. Fighting within the family is something you shouldn't tolerate. A house that is divided against itself cannot stand. Preserving unity is priority.

Please realize that being an all-star parent is a *process*. It's something you walk out one day at a time. Don't give up! Persevere. Dig into the Word of God and pray for wisdom. Study how others have done it. Someone else has already had the problem you are facing and has solved it. Each child is different, and every new phase they enter brings new challenges. Don't forget that the most important characteristic of an all-star parent is *establishing a good spiritual foundation* in your life and the lives of your children. God is the greatest parenting coach of all time, and He will show you how to apply these principles daily.

**TAKE AWAY**

- WHAT ARE THE TOP 3 NUGGETS OF WISDOM YOU CAN TAKE AWAY FROM THIS CHAPTER?
- WHAT PRINCIPLES ARE YOU ALREADY DOING?
- WHICH ONES DO YOU NEED TO PRAY AND ASK GOD TO HELP YOU PUT INTO PRACTICE?

---

**PARENTING 101 RECAP**: An all-star parent: (1) Establishes a strong spiritual foundation in their life and their children's lives. (2) Studies and continues to improve themselves as a person and a parent. (3) Becomes immune to the criticism of others. (4) Gives up being liked by their kids in exchange for being respected. (5) Recognizes bad behavior in all its forms and expects obedience. (6) Becomes an expert at creating fun-filled family moments. (7) Teaches their kids to appreciate and value family members and history.

# Chapter 8

# *Never Underestimate the Power of Prayer*

"…The earnest (heartfelt, continued) prayer of a righteous man makes tremendous power available [dynamic in its working]."

— James 5:16 AMP

We have presented many practical and proven principles and guidelines on parenting in this book. However, you cannot do any of them on your own. You need God to put them into practice. As you stay connected with Him in relationship, He promises to give you all the wisdom and strength you need to succeed at parenting your kids, and the way you stay connected is through *prayer*.

Prayer is powerful! Jesus said it can move mountains, and through it He raised the dead.[1] It can change our perspective, our attitude, and our situations and transform the lives of our children. Scripture says, "...The earnest (heartfelt, continued) prayer of a righteous man makes tremendous power available [dynamic in its working]" (James 5:16 AMP). Let's take a look at prayer and see how we, as parents, can make the most of this incredible gift God has given us

## WHAT IS PRAYER?

Simply put, prayer is talking and listening to God. It includes thanking Him, praising Him, and singing to Him. It is ongoing communication and friendship with God. It is not an activity we do just once a week on Sunday morning. It should be a natural part of your life – like breathing. Think about how often you interact with your closest friends. You talk on the phone, text, or email them every day. Why? Because you love them, they are an important part of your life, and you earnestly want to stay in touch. It's no different with God, and prayer is the vital link that keeps you connected.

Jesus Christ gives us the right to approach God's throne in prayer and ask for help to raise our kids. It is not something we can earn on our own. It is what Christ has already done for us. Ephesians 2:18 (NLT) says, "Now all of us can come to the Father through the same Holy Spirit because of what Christ has done for us." Jesus "...understands our weaknesses, for he faced all of the same temptations we do, yet *he did not sin*. So let us come boldly to the throne of our gracious God. There we will receive his mercy, and we will find grace to help us when we need it most" (Hebrews 12:15,16 NLT).

Prayer is both an act of *humility* and an act of *faith*. It is humility because it says by our actions, "God, I know I don't know it all, and I don't have the strength or the wisdom to do this without You." At the same time it is also faith, in that it shows by our actions that we believe God is real, He hears our prayers, and He is able and willing to answer them. As you stay connected with God in prayer, He will stay connected with you and give you the power and wisdom you need to be an outstanding parent.

> Prayer is simply talking and listening to God. It includes thanking Him, praising Him, and singing to Him. It is ongoing communication and friendship with God. It is not an activity we do just once a week on Sunday morning. It is a way of life.

## WHEN SHOULD YOU PRAY?

Ephesians 6:18 (TLB) tells us we are to "pray all the time. Ask God for anything in line with the Holy Spirit's wishes. Plead with him, reminding him of your needs, and keep praying earnestly for all Christians everywhere." And in 1 Thessalonians 5:17 we are told to "Never stop praying" (CEV). God doesn't want your prayer life to be like a fire extinguisher or a life preserver you reach for "in case of an emergency." He wants prayer to be an ongoing, loving communion between you and Him. You can come to Him anytime, anywhere, about anything. If you need wisdom on what to do in a situation, all you need to do is ask, and He will give it freely.[2]

No matter where you are—making breakfast, driving to work, or doing the dishes—you can pray. Not only can your pray for your kids, you can also pray for your country, your community, your coworkers, your friends, and yourself. The moment you begin to feel anxious, worried or fearful about something going on with your children or anything else, God wants you to turn to Him in prayer. He says, "Don't worry about anything; instead, *pray about everything*; tell God your needs and don't forget to thank him for his answers. If you do this you will experience God's peace, which is far more wonderful than the human mind can understand. His peace will keep your thoughts and your hearts quiet and at rest as you trust in Christ Jesus" (Philippians 4:6,7 TLB).

Wow! What a privilege prayer is. You can run to God anytime, anywhere, about anything and pour your heart out. Is your son being picked on at school? Pray for Him. Is your daughter struggling with insecurity and considering compromising her values to be accepted? Pray for her. Are you frustrated with yourself because you have been irritable and impatient with your kids and you cannot seem to overcome it? Pray. "The Lord says, 'I will rescue those who love me. I will protect those who trust in my name. When they call on me, I will answer; I will be with them in trouble. I will rescue and honor them'" (Psalm 91:14,15 NLT). God is ready, willing and able to give you His grace (strength) and His wisdom to handle any situation you face.

> God doesn't want your prayer life to be like a fire extinguisher or a life preserver you reach for "in case of an emergency." He wants prayer to be an ongoing, loving communion between you and Him. You can come to Him anytime, anywhere, about anything.

## HOW
## SHOULD YOU PRAY?

### PRAY WITH A HUMBLE, SINCERE HEART

The most important thing about prayer is not how long or loud you pray or even where you pray. The condition of your heart is what is most vital. While an attitude of pride *repels* God, an attitude of humility *attracts* Him.[3] He says, "...serve each other with humble spirits, for God gives special blessings to those who are humble, but sets himself against those who are proud" (1 Peter 5:5 TLB). In addition to humility, sincerity and reverence are also important. Scripture says, "The Lord is near to all who call upon Him, to all who call upon Him *sincerely* and in truth. He will fulfill the desires of those who reverently and worshipfully fear Him; He also will hear their cry and will save them" (Psalm 145:18,19 AMP). So praying to God with a humble, sincere heart of reverence is very important.

As far as your posture, there is no right or wrong position in which to pray. You can stand, sit, kneel, or lie with your face to the floor. Nevertheless, I do encourage people to fold their hands and bow their heads or raise their hands toward heaven as a sign of surrender. For me, these things show an attitude of humility toward God whose ears are open and attentive to my prayers.

> The most important thing about prayer is not how long or loud you pray or even where you pray. The condition of your heart is what is most vital. While an attitude of pride *repels* God, an attitude of humility *attracts* Him.

## PRAY GOD'S WORD

Another key element to include in your prayers is God's Word. In Isaiah 62:6 (AMP) God says, "...you who [are His servants and by your prayers] *put the Lord in remembrance [of His promises]*, keep not silence." God wants us to respectfully remind Him of what He has said in His Word. It's just like when your kids remind you of a promise you made to them. They say, "Hey Dad, you said that if we all got A's and B's in school this semester, you would take us out to eat this weekend. Remember? You promised...." In the same way, God wants us to remind Him of what He has promised us in His Word.

For example, let's say you are having some financial struggles. God doesn't want you to worry or be anxious about it. He wants you to *Pray*. You can say, "Lord, You said in Your Word that if we were faithful to give You our tithes and offerings, you would rebuke the devourer. You also said that if we give, You would give back to us and that You would supply all of our needs according to Your riches in glory.[4] Lord, You know my children and what their needs are. You know all the bills I need to pay. Please honor Your Word and provide for us. In Jesus name, Amen."

This is what it means to *put the Lord in remembrance of His promises.* We can do this in any situation we face. We can find out what God has promised us in His Word and make it a part of our prayers. Why is God's Word important? The main reason is because it is totally reliable. Numbers 23:19 (CEV) says, "God is no mere human! He doesn't tell lies or change his mind. *God always keeps his promises.*" Psalm 18:30 (NLT) echoes this truth, declaring "God's way is perfect. *All the Lord's promises prove true.* He is a shield for all who look to him for protection." And 1 Kings 8:56 (NLT) tells us that "...Not one word has failed of all the wonderful promises he gave through his servant Moses." This means we can pray for our children, speak God's Word over their lives, and He is going to honor it. He says, "...I am alert and active, watching over My word to perform it" (Jeremiah 1:12 AMP).

> God wants us to respectfully remind Him of what He has said in His Word. We can do this in any situation we face. We can find out what He has promised us in His Word and make it a part of our prayers.

## PRAY IN JESUS' NAME

In addition to praying with a humble and sincere heart and including God's Word, is the importance of praying "In Jesus' name." Now these are not just three magical words we whisper at the end of our prayer in order to get what we want from God. Saying "In Jesus' name" is putting Jesus' signature on our prayer request—it is as if Jesus Himself were here on earth asking the Father what we are requesting. Anything that Jesus would ask for, we can ask for. The key to knowing what He would ask for is being in relationship with Him and knowing His Word. He said, "If you *remain in me* and *my words remain in you*, you may ask for anything you want, and it will be granted!" (John 15:7 NLT).

To know God's Word is to know His will for us and our children. To pray His Word is to pray His will, and to pray His will is to experience His will. "This is the confidence we have in approaching God: that if we ask anything according to his will, he hears us. And if we know that he hears us—whatever we ask—we know that we have what we asked of him" (1 John 5:14,15 NIV). What promises can you find in Scripture that you can pray for your kids? Jesus says, "I will do

[I Myself will grant] whatever you ask in My Name [as presenting all that I AM], so that the Father may be glorified and extolled in (through) the Son" (John 14:13 AMP).

> Saying "In Jesus' name" is putting Jesus' signature on our prayer request—it is as if Jesus Himself were here on earth asking the Father what we are requesting. Anything that Jesus would ask for, we can ask for and it will be granted.

## PRAY EVERY KIND OF PRAYER REQUEST

The list of ways you can pray for your kids is endless. You can take virtually every verse of Scripture and turn it into a prayer. I believe that's what Paul means when he says, "Pray in the Spirit in every situation. *Use every kind of prayer and request there is.* ...Use every kind of effort and make every kind of request for all of God's people" (Ephesians 6:18 GW). If it's in the Bible, you can pray it. For example, you can pray for your kids to have a great relationship with God like Enoch, David, and Isaiah had.[5] You can pray for them to have great, godly friends and steer clear of bad company.[6] You can ask God to guide your children to make wise, godly choices.[7] You can pray they will yield themselves to Him and stay sexually pure.[8] You can pray for them to have great favor with God and man and a reverential fear of the Lord.[9]

One of the things Glori and I pray for our kids, is for them to find the godly spouse God has for them. We thank Him for the *one* marriage they will have to their great husband/wife.[10] We claim in prayer that the relationships we have with our sons-in-law and daughters-in-law will be just as loving and close as those we have with our sons and daughters. We also pray that our relationships with our future grandkids will be awesome. Again, the list of ways you can pray for your children is endless.

So take the promises of God's Word and pray them for your kids. As you're reading Scripture and you come across big, powerful principles and promises write them down and turn them into personalized prayers and proclamations for you and your children. If you have specific concerns and desires for them, open your Bible and search for verses regarding what God says on the subject. Take these issues to Him in prayer daily. If you are married, hold hands and pray with your spouse. If you are a single parent, pray with a trusted friend or relative. Jesus promises "...that when any two of you on earth agree about something you are praying for, my Father in heaven will do it for you" (Matthew 18:19 CEV). Indeed, the prayer of agreement unleashes exponential power into your situation.

> The list of ways you can pray for your kids is endless. You can take virtually every verse of Scripture and turn it into a prayer. If it's in the Bible, you can pray it. Take these issues to Him in prayer daily.

## WHY
## SHOULD YOU PRAY?

You may be thinking, *Mike, why should I pray? What's the big deal?* First and foremost, we should pray because God tells us to. Jesus didn't say *if* you pray—He said **when** you pray.[11] The second most important reason we should pray is that prayer is a powerful spiritual weapon against the enemy. As parents, we are in a war, and it is not against our kids or other people. It is a spiritual war against a spiritual enemy. Second Corinthians 10:3,4 (AMP) says, "For though we walk (live) in the flesh, we are not carrying on our warfare according to the flesh and using mere human weapons. For the weapons of our warfare are not physical [weapons of flesh and blood], but they are mighty before God for the overthrow and destruction of strongholds."

The enemy of our souls and spirits would like nothing more than to ruin our marriages, our children, our health, and everything else we hold dear. Thankfully, God has given us spiritual weapons to protect and defend our children and ourselves, and prayer is one of them. He doesn't want us to carry our weapons around as an idea in our head—He wants us to use them. Ephesians 6:10 in The Message Bible says, "…God is strong, and he wants you strong. So take everything the Master has set out for you, well-made weapons of the best materials. And put them to use so you will be able to stand up to everything the Devil throws your way. This is no afternoon athletic contest that we'll walk away from and forget about in a couple of hours. This is for keeps, a life-or-death fight to the finish against the Devil and all his angels."

As a Marine, I would never go into combat without my grenades and rifle. As a Christian, you should never go into a spiritual battle without your weapons. The spiritual weapons God gives us are stronger than anything the enemy can throw at us. Through Christ, God has already won the war and given us victory.[12] All we have to do is ask Him for grace and wisdom to use our weapons wisely and enforce what He has already done. The Scripture says, "He trains my hands for battle; he strengthens my arm to draw a bronze bow" (Psalm 18:34 NLT). God will fight through us when we yield ourselves to His leadership.

Not only has God given us effective spiritual weapons, He has also given us power and authority to use them. Jesus says, "Behold! I have given you *authority* and *power* to trample upon serpents and scorpions, and [physical and mental strength and ability] over *all* the power that the enemy [possesses]; and nothing shall in any way harm you" (Luke 10:19 AMP). God wants us to claim His power and use it in prayer. Don't think God is tired of hearing from you or that He is surprised at what is troubling or challenging you and your kids. He knows what is going to happen before it happens. He has given you power and authority over the enemy, and as you stay connected with Him, He will teach you how to win through the power of prayer.

> As parents, we are in a war, and it is not against our kids or other people. It is a spiritual war against a spiritual enemy. Thankfully, God has given us spiritual weapons to protect and defend our children and ourselves, and prayer is one of these powerful weapons.

# WHAT KEEPS GOD FROM HEARING YOUR PRAYERS?

Do you feel like God is not hearing your prayers or He is choosing not to answer them? It may be that something is hindering them. The number one thing that will keep God from hearing and answering your prayers is having sin in your life. Isaiah wrote, "Listen! The Lord's arm is not too weak to save you, nor is his ear too deaf to hear you call. It's your sins that have cut you off from God. Because of your sins, he has turned away and will not listen anymore" (59:1,2 NLT). If we have disobeyed God, we have sinned. "Whoever knows what is right but doesn't do it is sinning" (James 4:17 GW).

One of the most common sins that keeps God from hearing and answering prayer is holding onto unforgiveness. If there is an offense between you and one of your children or you and your spouse, your prayers will be hindered. Scripture says, "If you are a husband, you should be thoughtful of your wife. Treat her with honor, because she isn't as strong as you are, and she shares with you in the gift of life. Then nothing will stand in the way of your prayers" (1 Peter 3:7 CEV). Men, if you are in strife with your wife or your kids, your prayers are going to bounce off the ceiling. Ladies, the same is true for you. We must be willing to forgive one another of the hurts they cause, even as God has forgiven us.[13]

If you feel like something is hindering God from hearing your prayers, stop and ask Him to search your heart and reveal if any sin is there.[14] Ask Him to show you if there is anything you have done to displease Him or if you have left something undone that He asked you to do. If He shows you something specific, repent. That is the remedy for sin. First John 1:9 says, "God is faithful and reliable. If we confess our sins, he forgives them and cleanses us from everything we've done wrong." Once you repent, receive God's forgiveness, and go on. If you are dealing with unforgiveness, ask God to give you the grace to release the person and go on. If you wronged them, go apologize and make things right between the two of you.

> The number one thing that will keep God from hearing and answering your prayers is having sin in your life. If you feel like something is hindering God from hearing your prayers, stop and ask Him to search your heart and reveal if any sin is there.

## GOD ANSWERS PRAYER!

I can tell you from personal experience that God hears and answers prayer. There was an experience I had with our oldest son Austin that proved this to me. He was in his senior year of high school. He was receiving a number of scholarship offers for both academics and football. His team was number one in the district, and he was leading them in interceptions and fumble recoveries. As Austin and his team headed to the playoffs, he and our entire family were very excited by their success.

During the second to last game of the regular season, he was hit in the knee by another player as he was making a tackle. From the stands, I saw him wincing in pain and hopping on one leg. He immediately went back to his position to get ready for the next play, but when he realized he couldn't put any weight on his leg, he waved to his coach for permission to come out of the game – something he had never done before. That's when I knew he was hurt.

I quickly made my way out of the stands and jumped the fence to get to the sideline. The professional trainer who was there looking at Austin said, "His MCL is torn...gone...he's done." Knowing the power of words, I asked him to keep his comments to himself and not speak them to my son. I didn't want him planting negative seeds in his mind. (Review Chapter 2, *Harnessing the Power of Your Words*).

> "For the eyes of the Lord are on the righteous, and His ears are open to their prayers; but the face of the Lord is against those who do evil." —1 Peter 3:12 NKJV

Immediately, I began to *pray* silently, asking God to heal Austin and thanking Him for healing him. Meanwhile, Austin became despondent. I told him, "It'll be okay. Don't worry." Once the medical team fit him with a brace and gave him crutches, we went home. I continued to pray silently, asking for God's help like never before. Then I felt strongly impressed to pray for my son *out loud* so he could hear me. So I turned to him and said, "I believe God is going to heal you." I then put my hands on him and prayed for God to heal him. I said, "Lord, thank You for healing my son's knee. Thank You for reconnecting all the tissues and making everything healthy so that he can return to playing football. And thank You, Lord, for protecting my son. You are faithful and You will hear and answer our prayer. In Jesus' name, Amen."

I must be honest with you, I was a bit embarrassed. I didn't want Austin to think I was being weird or super spiritual. Nevertheless, because I wanted to obey what I felt God was telling me and see him healed, I prayed earnestly. I truly believe God healed him right then and there. By that night, the swelling was gone and there was no blood-bruising. When we went to the doctor on Monday to have an MRI done, it showed only a strain. None of the coaches or trainers could believe it, but Austin and I did. One week later, Austin was running and joined his team in their quest for the State Championship. Looking back, I believe the sideline trainer was right: My son's MCL was torn, and his knee was shot. But God in His grace and love and faithfulness restored it completely! He heard and answered the prayers of a father who stood in faith on the promises of God.

I know first-hand the power of prayer. God will hear you when you pray for your kids to return to Him, be healed, and overcome all of life's challenges. I can't promise you will experience a miraculous two-day turnaround, but somehow and some way, He will come through. He will give you the grace you need to overcome the challenges you are facing in your life and with your children. Trust Him.

> "The Lord says, 'I will rescue those who love me. I will protect those who *trust* in my name. When they call on me, I will answer; I will be with them in trouble. I will rescue and honor them." —Psalm 91:14,15 NLT

# PRAY
## AND GOD WILL MAKE THE IMPOSSIBLE POSSIBLE

Never underestimate the power of prayer! Keep searching the Scriptures and securing His promises that are for you and your children through Christ.

Personalize them and claim them for your family. By connecting with God in prayer and speaking His Word, you can break generational curses off your family. These are unhealthy habits and addictions that have been in your family line for years, such as rebellion, lying, fear, worry, gluttony, poverty, divorce, alcoholism, pornography, and every other bad habit or hang-up under the sun. Ask God for the blood of Christ to wash away those ungodly character traits and allow His Spirit to replace them with positive, godly ones.

Through faith in God's Word, prayer makes the impossible *possible*. Those dreams you have for your children and yourself can become a reality when you get God involved. Ephesians 3:20 in The Message says, "God can do anything, you know—far more than you could ever imagine or guess or request in your wildest dreams." So what are you praying and asking God to do for you and your children? Be bold and believe God for bigger and better things than you ever dreamed. Take Him at His Word

Through faith in God's Word, prayer makes the impossible *possible*. Those dreams you have for your children and yourself can become a reality when you get God involved.

Don't wait until your kids are in trouble to pray. Pray preemptive, proactive prayers. Thank God in advance for their academic excellence, diligence, and their heart to help others. Say things like, "Thank You, God, that my kids have the power to resist peer pressure and be respectful and obedient. I praise You that they are developing excellent, cheerful attitudes and that they love you with all their heart, soul, mind and strength." This is what God means when He says to call those things which do not exist as if they did.[15] If something disappointing or difficult happens to you or your kids, let prayer be your *first response*, not your last resort.

The next best thing to praying for your kids is to *teach them how to pray*. You can do this by letting them see and hear you pray. Don't worry if you haven't been good at praying or afraid that your kids will think you are weird. Just start off small and let it grow. Help them learn how to plug into God's power and establish a life-long communication with the

Creator of the universe. Give them feedback on how they are doing, and coach them on how to be thankful, offer praise and worship, and include Scripture in their prayers. Whenever the opportunity arises, point them back to God's Word and the importance of seeking Him for the answers they need. A solid relationship with God will carry them through their troubled times.

I challenge you to make the decision right now to partner with God and be the parent your kids need. Get God involved in every aspect of your life and their lives through prayer. Whatever you do, don't stop praying for your kids—even if they are grown and out of the house. Pray for them all the time, in every situation that arises.

Being a parent is a lifelong role. As your kids grow, your level of responsibility will change, but you are connected with them for life. May God give us the wisdom and grace we need to be the parents He wants us to be. May He show us how to raise our kids in such a way that we unlock their full potential and set them on the path of extraordinary success.

**TAKE AWAY**

- WHAT ARE THE TOP 3 NUGGETS OF WISDOM YOU CAN TAKE AWAY FROM THIS CHAPTER?
- WHAT PRINCIPLES ARE YOU ALREADY DOING?
- WHICH ONES DO YOU NEED TO PRAY AND ASK GOD TO HELP YOU PUT INTO PRACTICE?

---

**PARENTING 101 RECAP**: Prayer is powerful! It keeps us connected with God and releases His dynamic power into our lives and the lives of our children. Through Jesus Christ, we have the privilege to pray anytime, anywhere, about anything. When we pray, all that God asks of us is that we have a humble, sincere and reverent heart. So keep the lines of communication between you and God open. Don't let sin hinder your prayers. Pray God's Word in Jesus' name over you and your children, and He will make the impossible possible!

# How Can You Have a Personal Relationship with God?

Throughout our journey to become better parents, I have frequently talked about the importance of turning to God for help. It is only through a personal relationship with Him that you will have the ability to be a great parent and raise great kids. Without Him in your life, you cannot help connect your kids to God and establish a good spiritual foundation in their lives. Without Him, you are left to raise your children in your own strength and wisdom. The truth is, without Him you and I can do nothing.[1]

"Well, Mike, how can I have a personal relationship with God?" That's a good question. The answer is simple—**invite Him in**. He loves you and I so much He sent His Son, Jesus, to take our punishment for all the wrong we would ever do.[2] Jesus was perfect, without sin, and He died that our relationship with God might be restored.[3] When you *believe* and declare that Jesus Christ was God's Son, He lived a sinless life, died to pay for your sins, and rose from the grave to give you power to live right, you are born into His family.[4] Your relationship with Him is restored and His Spirit comes to live in your heart.[5]

Are you ready to invite God in? Then pray this simple prayer aloud from your heart:

*God, I come to you just as I am. I know I have done many things wrong. I am sorry for my sins. Please forgive me and wash me clean on the inside with the life-giving blood of Jesus.*[6] *Come and live in my heart. Give me wisdom and strength to be a godly parent and live a life that pleases You.*[7] *I don't understand everything about being born into Your family, but I know I need You. Thank You for loving me and sending Jesus to die in my place and pay the penalty for my sin. Thank You for forgiving me and coming into my heart and showing me how to live. In His Name I pray, Amen.*

If you prayed that prayer, you are now a child of God! Welcome to the family! The angels in heaven are standing and cheering at what you just did.[8] God loves you so much and is now living in your heart. You have access to everything you need to grow and mature into an all-star parent.[9]

Is there a friend or family member you know who has a relationship with God? Give them a call and tell them about your decision for God. You will excite them beyond words. We would also love to hear from you. Shoot us an email at mikestorms101@gmail.com. We want to celebrate with you and help you get started in your new Christian life.

**Scriptures for Personal Study**:

(1) See John 15:5. (2) See John 3:16,17. (3) See 2 Corinthians 5:21; Hebrews 4:14-16.
(4) See Romans 10:9,10. (5) See John 14:23; 1 John 3:24. (6) See 1 John 1:9.
(7) See James 1:5; Psalm 32:8. (8) See Luke 15:10. (9) See 2 Peter 2:3.

# Notes

## Chapter 1

(1) http://blog.nielsen.com/nielsenwire/media_entertainment/tv-viewing-among-kids-at-an-eight-year-high/, retrieved 11-13-10.
(2) http://www.thedailygreen.com/environmental-news/latest/kids-television-47102701, retrieved 11-13-10.
(3) See Matthew 5:3-10
(4) See Philippians 4:11-13
(5) See 2 Corinthians 6:14,15 The Message.
(6) See Matthew 12:33-35.
(7) See John 15:5
(8) See Deuteronomy 6:7.

## Chapter 2

(1) See Genesis 1:27; Ephesians 5:1.
(2) Colossians 4:6 NIV
(3) Philippians 4:13

## Chapter 3

(1) See Psalm 145:8,9; Micah 7:18.
(2) See 2 Samuel 22:31
(3) See John 14:26.
(4) See Romans 12:21.
(5) Proverbs 11:27 NIV.
(6) See Romans 15:13.

## Chapter 4

(1) See Ephesians 6:12,13; 2 Corinthians 10:3,4.
(2)See Romans 3:23
(3)See John 15:5; Philippians 4:13

## Chapter 5

(1) See James 1:17.
(2) See Matthew 6:14,15.
(3) See Hebrews 1:3.
(4) See John 14:23; Revelation 3:20; 1 John 3:24.
(5) See John 16:13; Psalm 32:8.
(6) See Psalm 25:12.
(7) See Proverbs 3:5-7.

## Chapter 6

(1) See Romans 14:12.
(2) See Ephesians 4:15.

## Chapter 7

(1) See Romans 1:20.
(2) See James 1:27.
(3) See Proverbs 12:15.
(4) See Romans 14:12.
(5) See Proverbs 3:5,6.
(6) See Proverbs 6:16,17; Psalm 51:6.
(7)See John 16:13
(8)See Mark 3:25
(9)See Ephesians 4:3

## Chapter 8

(1) See Mark 11:23; John 11:41-43.
(2) See James 1:5.
(3) See Isaiah 66:2; James 4:6.
(4) See Malachi 3:10,11; Luke 6:38; Philippians 4:19.
(5) See Genesis 5:22-24, Psalm 27:4, 8; Isaiah 26:9.
(6) See Proverbs 13:20, 1 Corinthians 15:33.
(7) See Psalm 25:4,5, 9, 12, 32:8; John 16:13, James 1:5.
(8) See Job 31:1; Psalm 119:9; Proverbs 5; Ephesians 5:3; 1 Corinthians 6:18; 1Thessalonians 4-7.
(9) See Genesis 6:8,9; Psalm 5:12, Proverbs 3:3,4; Psalms 111:10, Proverbs 1:7, Proverbs 10:27, Proverbs 14:26,27.
(10) See Proverbs 5:18,19; Proverbs 18:22; 2 Corinthians 6:14,15.
(11) See Matthew 6:5-7.
(12) See Romans 8:37.
(13) See Ephesians 4:32.
(14) See Psalm 139:23,24.
(15) See Romans 4:17.

# About the Author

Mike Storms is one of those authorities that parents gravitate to, when it comes to equipping families and kids with the tools they need to succeed. From sharing rock solid parenting tips to building confidence in kids and helping marriages last, Mike has spent years providing time-tested advice that really works!

Mike is the popular author of Safer Smarter Kids, as well as a number of other resources, workbooks and guides that have benefited thousands of people worldwide. His latest book, Parenting 101, with a supporting workbook, is set to be released this spring at Book Expo America.

With a unique, hands-on style, that comes from Mike's 30+ years teaching and coaching over 6,000 children. Though his Louisiana based martial arts school, where he is a 7th degree black belt and karate master, and using the disciple and training that a foundation in martial arts provides, Mike is able to deliver advice that gets results.

He is also a well-known speaker who has appeared at events with such popular and respected author-motivators as Mark Victor Hansen, Dan Kennedy, and Brian Tracy. Mike is a veteran of the US Marines, and has served as martial arts instructor to the New Orleans Saints, University of Virginia, Tulane University, and the North Carolina Tarheels.

Mike resides in Mandeville, Louisiana with his wife, Glori. and their 4 children.

For more information and to sign up for Mike's free parenting and family tips, visit: www.MikeStorms.me

*If you found this book thought provoking and would like to have Mike Storms speak to your organization, please feel free to contact him at:*


Mike Storms

*mikestorms101@gmail.com*
*www.MikeStorms.me*

PRESS LLC

*www. focusonethics.com*
*www.dcpressbooks.com*